WildBlue Press
TRUE CRIME
features

KEVIN SULLIVAN
VAMPIRE
The Richard Chase Murders

WildBluePress.com

VAMPIRE published by:
WILDBLUE PRESS
1153 Bergen Pkwy Ste I #114
Evergreen, Colorado 80439

Copyright 2014 by Kevin Sullivan

All rights reserved. No part of this book may be reproduced in any form or by any means without the prior written consent of the Publisher, excepting brief quotes used in reviews.

WILDBLUE PRESS is registered at the U.S. Patent and Trademark Offices.

eBook ISBN: 978-1-942266-06-8
Trade Paperback ISBN: 978-1-942266-11-2

*This book is dedicated to the victims of Richard Trenton Chase, both the living and the dead,
And to those who captured him and stopped the killing.*

Other WildBlue Press Books By Kevin Sullivan

KENTUCKY BLOODBATH: *Ten Bizarre Tales of Murder From the Bluegrass State*
http://wbp.bz/kb

THE TRAIL OF TED BUNDY: *Digging Up The Untold Stories*
http://wbp.bz/trailbundy

THE BUNDY SECRETS: *Hidden Files On America's Worst Serial Killer*
http://wbp.bz/bundysecrets

Preface

Richard Trenton Chase was born on May 23, 1950. To all outward appearances, he was a normal baby, filled with the normal smiles and reactions that capture the love and hearts of those around them. What could not be seen, however, was the dark strand running through the child, who would, after a series of events, drastically alter the lives of many people unfortunate enough to cross paths with the one who ultimately became known as "The Vampire of Sacramento."

Like all killers who prey upon the innocent, the desire to use and then destroy people (or destroy them prior to use) was present within Richard Chase and spoke of his fractured personality. His thinking was both extremely abnormal and wholly sociopathic. Like the American serial killer, Theodore Bundy, Chase had absolutely no compunction at the taking of human life. Unlike Theodore Bundy, however, Chase was delusional as to his own person and what he needed to sustain his life. Bundy was a sexual sadist. He reveled in the destruction of women and enjoyed having sex with his victims while they were alive and after death, as well. He wore a mask of sanity for the outside world, and those who knew him saw only a handsome and articulate young man who had a good future ahead of him in either law or politics. Richard Chase, on the other hand, had no mask to hide behind, reached a place in early adulthood where he could not interact with the outside world, was filthy as to his person, and clearly presented an image of mental illness. Both were diabolical killers, yet both were radically different per outward image.

Although legally sane (as would be aptly demonstrated during his trial), Chase was viewed as a sick fiend by the public, and one whose crimes were borne out of a psychotic mind. To all who dealt with him, from the investigators who hunted him, to the attorneys who prosecuted or defended him, and the medical community charged with diagnosing him, Richard Chase was clearly a demented individual who lived outside the norms of society and proved himself to be a lethal entity to those he attacked. That society failed to see this extreme and violent predatory nature beginning to blossom in Richard Chase is not surprising at all, for as Chase degenerated into an individual obviously suffering from mental illness, such illnesses rarely produce the kind of homicidal rampage produced by his hands.

So, when a quiet area of Sacramento, California, was turned upside down through a series of grisly murders, and it was realized that the murderer was clearly operating in a geographically small area, it became a daunting challenge for law enforcement to apprehend the one responsible. That the perpetrator was a disorganized killer, giving little thought to whom he struck or when he struck, and not taking the kind of precautions of those who plan their murders, their task of finding the madman was made only slightly easier. In the end, the lives of six people would be extinguished because of his actions, and many, many more (the living victims) would be emotionally altered forever. For these unfortunates, life will always be defined as the time before Richard Chase and the time afterward. Words and circumstances can never change what was, and the only bright spot in this case is that Richard Chase was caught before he could kill more.

It is my intention in this book to write the full story of the Richard Chase murders: From his early beginnings and the family environment in which he grew into manhood, to the torturing of animals (so common in murderers), and to his eventual mental disintegration and launch into murder. But, it also is the story of the victims, those murdered and those left to deal with the heavy emotional toll. These lives, both the dead and the living, have a voice here, as well. No longer will they be names only, but will be revealed for the people they were, and how terribly their lives were altered.

An interesting postscript to the actual beginning of my journey to tell the story of the Richard Chase murders starts with our arrival in Sacramento, California. Having taken an Amtrak passenger train, we arrived in the city around 9:00 p.m. on January 30, 2012, a good six hours later than expected due to a fire on the train in Hastings, Nebraska. Gathering our luggage, we took a taxi to our hotel, and as my wife entered the lobby to register us, I helped the driver unload our things and quickly tipped him so he could leave. As the cabbie made a U-turn and headed back to the train station for additional passengers, I grabbed two suitcases and headed for the hotel's front door. As I did so, I heard someone calling out to me. Turning around, I rested the suitcases on the pavement and watched a disheveled young man with dark hair approaching me. Bathed in the artificial light of the parking lot, I could see he appeared very much like the Richard Chase of 1978. When I asked him what he wanted (I thought it would be money), he wanted to know if I had a cigarette. I told him no, explaining that I didn't smoke. With that, a rather strange look spread across his face, and he turned and walked away. As I watched him go, he let out a strange howl and moved his body oddly.

That episode was the beginning of this book.

A note to readers: All quotations in this work are from the files of the Sacramento County District Attorney and are part of the original investigative file and court documents pertaining to the Richard Chase murders. There are four quotations from *Dracula Killer*, (Biondi and Hecox), several quotes from *The Sacramento Bee* and *The Sacramento Union* and one quote from Investigation Discovery's *Twisted* documentary of Richard Chase, as well as phone and e-mail communications with individuals connected to the case.

Chapter One

First Blood

Thursday, December 29, 1977, had been a completely uneventful day in the lives of most Sacramentans. But what was about to happen was just the beginning of a nightmare for the people of the capital city of Sacramento, and a very personal nightmare for one particular family. Ambrose Griffin, fifty-one, an engineer with the Bureau of Land Management, had just returned from the grocery store with his wife, Carol. As they pulled into the driveway of their home at 3734 Robertson Avenue, it was a little before 8:30 p.m., and all was apparently quiet. Handing her the keys, Ambrose told his wife to unlock the trunk, and as she did so, Carol grabbed the sack of potatoes, while her husband curled a bag with each arm. Gail Griffin, the Griffins' daughter-in-law, was by this time holding the front door open, so that the task of unloading would take only a matter of minutes. Placing the two bags of groceries down on the kitchen counter, Ambrose Griffin naturally headed back outside to retrieve the last bag. And after clearing the front door, it was only a matter of chance that he would be walking towards his car at the precise moment when a person bent on killing someone would be driving past his house. Gail Griffin, who had momentarily turned away from the door and was looking back into the house, had seen a car driving down the street, but thought nothing of it. Now was the moment. After spotting his unsuspecting victim, the man pushed the barrel of a .22 caliber pistol out the driver's side window. Two quick squeezes of the trigger, and the Luger-style, semi-automatic handgun fired twice, its shell casings landing and bouncing on the pavement below. The killer, who had been travelling east on Robertson Avenue, then sped away. As soon as she heard the shots, Gail Griffin turned and saw her father-in-law having trouble, and he may have already been lying on the ground. (It is important to note here some minor discrepancies within the police records concerning statements made by family members, who obviously were under an extreme amount of stress and pressure due to the horrific events confronting them. For example, Gail Griffin, who was holding open the door for her in-laws, states as she looked back, she saw her father-in-law on the ground. Carol Griffin, however, remembered it slightly differently. There also is the possibility of an error being made by a uniformed patrol officer conducting the first interviews).

Vampire

Ambrose Griffin home the evening of the shooting

Inside, Carol Griffin and her son, David, who was on the phone talking with a friend, also heard two shots, and these would later be described by Carol as "backfires" or "pops," and she did not associate them with gunfire. David Griffin told investigators the noise sounded like a car backfiring. As she exited the front door and moved onto the porch, Carol Griffin caught sight of her husband, standing with his back toward her, next to the car. He then turned around and fell to the ground. Ambrose Griffin, still barely conscious, was able to tell his wife "I have been shot." Despite this, Mrs. Griffin believed her husband must have suffered a heart attack. At this time, Gail Griffin and her brother-in-law, David, covered Ambrose with blankets and tried to keep him from moving.

The wailing of an ambulance siren could be heard approaching the Griffin home on Robertson Avenue. The family, still believing this was the result of a heart attack, was taken aback when the paramedics on the scene pulled back his jacket to reveal a spreading blood stain on his shirt. Ambrose Griffin was now in a fight for his life, and within moments, the medical team from Superior Ambulance Service was speeding him to the American River Hospital. The departing ambulance would soon be replaced by the arrival of police vehicles once it was learned that a shooting had occurred, and the investigators, whose job it was to discover the one responsible for the shooting, would be hampered from the start by the lack of evidence in what they believed might be a motiveless crime. Bill Roberts, a rookie detective at the time, recently told me what it was like working that case: "I kept thinking, 'This is a quiet neighborhood near Carmichael; stuff like this doesn't happen here.' ... It just didn't make sense that a man was shot while unloading groceries from a car. We didn't even call this a drive-by shooting. The term was relatively new and almost exclusively used in talking about Los Angeles. Not Sacramento." Later, Bill Roberts would come face-to-face with the reason all of this had happened.

As Ambrose Griffin was wheeled into the emergency room at American River Hospital, a paramedic was administering CPR, and it was hoped that a spark of life was still within him. But, the damage done to this husband and father of three was beyond repair. According to police reports, "Blood pressure upon admission was 40/0 and attended by doctors Ledwich and Ferror. Chest tube number thirty-two and number sixteen Foley Cath (sic) inserted by Doctor Ledwich. IV cut downs performed left arm, left foot. One unit whole blood administered. Subject was admitted at 2052 hours and was pronounced expired by Doctor Ledwich at 2125 hours."

As the family arrived at the hospital, they were informed their loved one was dead. It was unthinkable that out of nowhere, something so horrible and life-altering could have happened to them, but it did, and now they were forced to cope with the terrible reality. By the time homicide detectives arrived at the hospital, the family had returned home. They did, however, have a chance to make a statement to a patrol officer by the name of Firenza prior to leaving the hospital.

As detectives viewed the body of Mr. Griffin, they made the following remarks: "Subject was observed lying supine on hospital gurney in treatment room, nude, and covered with a sheet. Subject was lying on partially cut-off clothing, black-white plaid sport shirt, black sweater, white T-shirt, and print-colored boxer shorts. Surgical-type open incision noted upper left chest area, to left of midline and above left nipple, also right chest below and to the right of right nipple." According to the pathologist, Doctor Pierce Rooney Jr., the shot that killed Ambrose Griffin "entered the anterior of the right chest. It had a slightly downward trajectory, with virtually no deviation from right to left, and went through the lung and diaphragm."

It was an unlikely murder in an unlikely neighborhood, and currently, it was beyond explanation. It also was the culmination of a series of shootings in this quiet enclave of homes over the past few weeks. As investigators canvassed the neighborhood, they heard stories that would later be directly connected to the murder of Ambrose Griffin. Edward and Irene Stolz lived two doors down from the Griffins, at 3738 Robertson Avenue. On the evening of the murder, Edward Stolz told authorities he heard what he believed to be the discharging of two .22-caliber bullets and the sound of a car passing by. His wife, he said, heard nothing, as she was in the rear portion of their home. But this was not the only information Edward Stolz had for police. He also reported that around 2:00 a.m. on the 22nd of December as he was taking out the garbage cans to the road, he heard the sound of "a large-caliber shot" being fired and saw what he believed to be a light-colored vehicle passing by his house. Stolz confessed to detectives that he had difficulty seeing, as he wasn't wearing his glasses at that hour.

It is important to note that, on occasion, gun shots could be heard in the vicinity of the creek running directly behind Robertson Avenue. This usually would be the result of those believing that shooting guns into the creek (plinking, as it's known to the participants) is perfectly acceptable — so much so, that no matter how annoying it might have been to the residents, it was rarely reported to the police; but, neither did it ever result in the near-killing of an individual or a peppering of their homes. What was happening now was far different.

Hugh K. Phares, an instructor at American River College, lived with his wife, Marguerite, at 3804 Robertson Avenue, but had never met Ambrose Griffin. Living on the same side of Robertson as the Griffins, some four or five houses to the west, he told investigators he did not hear shooting that night and only learned of the terrible event the next morning. He did, however, report that on "Christmas Day, December 25, 1977, Sunday morning between 10:00 and 12:00 noon…" he heard as many as six shots fired from the area of the creek, but couldn't see anything because of the surrounding shrubbery. And again, on the 26th or 27th of December, he heard more firing around 11:00 p.m. Being in the upstairs bathroom at the time, he had trouble ascertaining the direction the shooting was coming from, except to say it was between: "Watt Avenue, Robertson Avenue, Montclaire Street, and Marconi Avenue."

On January 7, 1978, the sound of occasional gunshots reverberating past their house would take on an intensely personal tone, when Phares would discover "gypsum plaster dust" on some boxes being stored in an infrequently used closet off their living room. What seemed strange to Hugh Phares was the dust being present, as he had been in the closet recently and knew the boxes were clean. On closer inspection, he noticed a spent, copper-coated bullet lying on the top shelf. Connecting the dots, Phares knew what happened and soon found the entrance hole in the closet, the corresponding hole in the living room, and the hole in the wall of the front of the house facing Robertson Avenue. Investigators would soon determine the bullet entered the front wall near the fireplace, ricocheted off the living room ceiling, and bored its way through the living room wall and into the closet, where it finally came to rest.

At the nearby Polenske home on Lynn Way, Mrs. Polenske was busy one early evening cleaning her kitchen, when a bullet smashed through the window, whizzed through her hair, and slammed into the wall. It was 6:30 p.m. December 27, 1977, and it would be sometime before investigators learned the connection between this incident, the shooting at the Phares residence, and the murder of Ambrose Griffin.

Lieutenant Ray Biondi, chief of the homicide division at the Sacramento County Sheriff's Department, received a call at his home about the Griffin killing within thirty minutes of the shooting. Little did he realize that answering this call (and being forced once again to head out into the night, when he'd prefer to stay home) would be far more than just responding to a singular and tragic homicide, for what had just been unleashed was but the beginning of an investigation unlike anything Sacramentans had thus far experienced.

Unfortunately for police, it would be a scene with very little evidence, and it wouldn't be long before detectives determined that Ambrose Griffin was a stable family man who had no known enemies. There was absolutely no known reason why anyone would want to kill him. And, it appeared that the perpetrator had merely killed Mr. Griffin in a drive-by shooting. The next twenty-four hours (and beyond) would mean plenty of leg-work for the detectives and patrol officers alike, who canvassed the neighborhood around the Griffin home, talking to everyone about what they may have seen or heard in their quest to locate good solid leads. Because Mr. Griffin had been shot at night, it would be impossible to do a thorough search of the grounds for any real evidence at that time, and it didn't matter how many cops you had on the scene. The illumination of the day was important for the work before them.

Unfortunately, it would be a television news crew who would stumble upon the .22-caliber shell casings lying in the street some eighty feet west of the Griffin home. One of the shell casings was undamaged, but one had been almost completely flattened by a vehicle rolling over it. That the casings had been carried so far from the site of the shooting was at first a mystery. Later, however, investigators concluded the shells ejected onto the hood of the shooter's car and were carried that far before rolling off into the street. In any event, it was the only physical evidence authorities had of the killing. The hunt for his murderer had begun, but finding the one responsible would not be easy. As any homicide detective will tell you: Murder without motive is one of the most difficult crimes to solve. Those given the task of solving this case would not have to wait long for connecting evidence. Unfortunately, this evidence would come only after additional and more horrific murders would be committed. And, the people of Sacramento, California, would soon hear things that would make even the most hardened person shudder.

Chapter Two

Growing up Strange

Richard Trenton Chase was born on May 23, 1950, in Sacramento, California, only nine-and-one-half months after his parents, Richard and Beatrice, were married. The world in which Richard was born was good and was trending upwards. In the United States, this was a period of growth, both economically and in population. The Second World War had devastated the planet, and the generation that survived the war that ended in 1945 was determined to birth life back into the world, thereby creating what we have come to know in the United States as the Baby Boom generation of 1946 through 1964. It was a time of immense opportunity for the country. But, every family, like every individual, is unique, and while the home life helped shape the personality of Richard Chase, other factors would come into play in making him what he ultimately became. Things would not go well as the years rolled along.

In 1952, Richard Sr. acquired a federal position as a computer specialist at McClellan Air Force

Base, while Beatrice taught school. The following year, Pamela Chase was born, and the same year the family moved into their first house on Kings Way and remained there until 1961, at which time they moved to a home on Wheat Street. This home, however, they lost to "financial troubles caused in part by marital problems." For the next two years, the family lived in a duplex on Valkyrie Way, until they purchased a home on Montclaire Street. And, while money was apparently never again a major problem in the Chase home, other cracks would appear in the family between Beatrice and Richard Sr. According to court reports, as early as 1962, serious problems were occurring between the two, with "many loud arguments" and charges from Mrs. Chase that her husband was using "dope and of infidelity." She even accused him on two occasions of "poisoning her." Although Richard Sr. would admit to authorities that he sometimes drank too much and even had had problems handling money, he must have found this last charge very strange indeed. Certainly, with what was to come from his son, it may have taken on a special meaning as time passed. As for young Richard, for the first eight years of his life, he seemed quite normal. A Cub Scout, he enjoyed playing in Little League (four years) and had the normal range of friends and activities. During the sixth grade, some fifty children showed up for his birthday party, and all went well. So, whatever was churning inside him was, at least for the present time, hidden from view. That which would ultimately surface would do so in the years ahead and would become evident to those around him at that time. However, no one could have imagined what was coming and what terrible things would transpire by his hands.

Discipline in the Chase home was, for the most part, carried out by the father, as Beatrice admitted she tended to be lenient with the children. Pamela confirmed this, saying her father was "strict" and sometimes things would get physical between the two. On one occasion when Richard was two, Mr. Chase force-fed his son, which caused him to vomit. Other confrontations between Mr. Chase and his son were given and have become part of the official record, confrontations where he would "shake" the child or was accused of pitching him into a wall. Mr. Chase also admitted yelling at him when Richard was about eleven after the boy (apparently accidently) locked the keys in the car.

As the years inched forward, marital life would turn even darker at the Montclaire household. More accusations of infidelity would surface, as Beatrice believed her husband was "having an affair with their neighbor ... of having women in their yard." When the family vacationed in Oregon on a camping trip, Mrs. Chase confronted him about having a woman waiting in the woods. The trip ruined, the family returned home to Sacramento. Oddly, she spoke of her husband "annoying her at night in bed ... claims she must have been drugged for him to be able to do this."

In 1965, Beatrice took the kids south to Los Angeles, but Mr. Chase came down after eight days and retrieved Richard. Mrs. Chase remained in Los

Angeles another four months before returning home. That the marriage had not yet completely disintegrated is amazing. Even so, Beatrice and Richard Chase Sr. separated for the last time in June of 1972, and the divorce was finalized on January 2, 1973.

Beatrice Chase later explained to investigators how difficult things were with Richard even at the early age of thirteen: "(He was) trying to cook for himself. He burnt pans, and he would leave stuff all over it and big puddles on the floor. He never picked up or cleaned anything. Now, he was up stewing around and cooking (and) burning stuff all night long, and it got to be vexing ... we couldn't sleep, my daughter and I in the house. He'd turn the PGE (Pacific Gas & Electric) on, and he'd turn it up so high, open the windows (and) let the heat out, and strip off (all his clothes), lying on the couch in the living room."

It was about this same time Richard started thinking he was one of the Younger Brothers of Western fame. So, "he checked a book out of the library, and he got a poster made, and he had his picture pasted in the picture for one of the Younger Brothers. Now, he later on had some big poster a whole bunch of them and was trying to sell them ... he (also) wanted a cowboy hat and all that, and he wanted a red handkerchief, which I did not buy him a cowboy hat, but he wanted one."

In September of 1964, Richard Chase entered Mira Loma High School. At this time, he was still exhibiting a normal personality. Those who knew him speak of a well-groomed person, fairly popular, who had the normal interaction with friends, both male and female, and this continued for the next couple of years. His grades at this time were slightly below average — C's and D's — but by his sophomore year, F's started to appear on his report cards. The desire to be more than just friends with the opposite sex was rising within him, as well, but like the downturn in his grades, this area began to unravel very quickly. Always exceedingly thin (Chase did not like this about himself), he was about to enter the world of dating.

In 1965, Richard Chase began a relationship with Libby Christopher (a pseudonym). She was a couple of years behind Richard and apparently liked him, as they continued dating into 1966. However, the sexual relationship never progressed beyond the preliminary stages of foreplay, as Chase was never able to maintain an erection. While this did not immediately drive Libby away, it was the catalyst over time in making her decision to break off the relationship. Of course, whatever feelings of inferiority or insecurity he may have been experiencing prior to the breakup, these would be multiplied many times over after this occurred. He would continue to date, but his inability to provide what was expected of him did not go away, and his dysfunction soon became common knowledge among his peers.

It was during this time of emotional upheaval that Chase began to experiment heavily with drugs: marijuana, LSD, and on occasion, amphetamines. Not surprisingly, Chase's disposition began to change greatly, and others (including family members) remember him as being rude, inconsiderate and slovenly in appearance, and that he started letting his hair grow out. 1965 also saw his first brush with the law, when he was nabbed with marijuana. The arrest obviously caused his father to be angry, and the two would argue about drugs even while the son denied taking any. Their arguments also were about Richard's lack of hygiene and what the father perceived (correctly) as his son's lack of drive and aimless approach to life. What Mr. Chase could not perceive were the dark impulses that had not yet reached the surface. To the outsider, these types of arguments were in fact occurring in many homes across the nation during those years, as the generation gap between parents and children widened in the 1960s. But Richard was no ordinary rebellious child of the time. Richard Chase was a mentally disturbed, diabolical killer-in-the-making; a homicidal time bomb waiting to explode on the unsuspecting people of Sacramento.

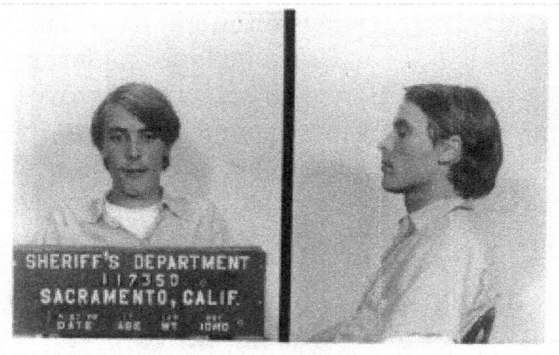

The first arrest of Richard Chase

December 1971 arrest

On June 6, 1968, Richard Chase graduated from Mira Loma High School, and for this accomplishment, his parents bought him a Volkswagen as a graduation present. Graduating high school is a line of demarcation for young people. No matter if it's off to college or on to a sales position, the military, or some other endeavor, leaving school is the first step into adulthood. And, with it comes the natural pressures associated with living. Although the descent into darkness had already begun for Richard Chase, he nevertheless decided to enroll in college. And, this he did in September of 1968. Chase would stay a student at American River College until the spring semester of 1971, at which time he "took a leave of absence." Of course, his schooling could not, and did not, alter his bizarre thinking, and he saw a psychiatrist for the first time in 1969 for his inability to sustain an erection. He also was employed for a brief period in 1969 with Retailers Credit Association, which involved typing and phone work, and according to his mother, he "did a very good job." There would be other menial jobs, of course, but Chase could never keep them long, as the drugs and the mental deterioration had taken its toll. Even so, he was not yet a danger to humans.

Although Chase began college while living at his Montclaire residence, he'd soon move into a house at 3831 Anadale Lane with Cyd Evans DeMarchi and Rachel Statum. The two had found Chase sitting on the front lawn on a day in February 1971, and the three began to talk. As Chase was not drooling and babbling incoherently, DeMarchi and Statum had no idea what a mistake this was going to be, but they soon would find out. Once ensconced in the house (Richard's father gave him fifty dollars each month for rent, and Chase worked odd jobs to make ends meet), Chase was always "stoned" and was often "uncooperative, inconsiderate, (and) difficult to be with." Chase, obviously driven by paranoia, boarded up the door to his room, knocked a hole into the closet wall so that he could enter and exit his room, and made his abode a fortress as best as he could. His reason for doing so, he said, was so that "no one can sneak up on me." One day, DeMarchi watched as Chase leaned out a window and started waving a gun at someone coming up the walk. Soon after this, DeMarchi and Statum had had enough, and they asked Chase to leave. He refused, so they moved out. Rachel Statum's brothers and some of their friends, however, moved right in, and soon they, too, were having problems with Richard Chase. Apparently, the brothers and friends were in a rock band, and Chase, not content to just listen, joined them in practice, playing a conga drum and singing. He was "no good," they would later tell investigators, and they tried talking Chase out of playing with them. But, that would produce arguments, and he'd "join in" anyway. Add to this his constant bizarre actions, being high all the time and walking out of his bedroom nude while the guys had girls over. All of this made for an intolerable situation, and soon, Richard Chase would be back with his mother on Montclaire Street.

Whatever problems Chase had were, of necessity, shared by the family. In these situations, it can be no other way. Unlike those who merely came in contact with this very odd person, people who could shudder and turn away, the family had to be there, and as such, would suffer their own mental anguish. They would also be forced to take up the slack when it came to providing for him financially. One area that was an absolutely useless drain of resources was the traffic tickets Chase had a penchant for racking up. According to his mother, at one point, he had as many as fifteen tickets, and as a result, lost his license. Chase then bought a motorcycle. Even before this, he'd sold the Volkswagen he'd received at graduation and purchased an old Ford, but for now the motorcycle would have to do.

In 1972, Chase took a trip alone to Utah. He was

only gone about two weeks, but he was arrested while there for yet another traffic violation. His car was impounded, and his two dogs were temporarily placed in a shelter. While there, Chase said the officers "gassed him," that he was now ill and wanted to sue the police, but his father talked him out of it. "He had two dogs," Beatrice explained. "He had a little fluffy white dog (Sabbath), and he had Heavy. And Heavy was a German Sheppard. So I sent him some money, and when he got back he had a string of tickets a mile long, and I put out eighty-one dollars in tickets." She also said he "acted crazy ... acted completely berserk. And I said what happened, and he said ... 'I think they gave me something in jail or asphyxiated me some way.' He'd have fits. He beat his feet into the wall, and it was just awful." When asked if her son could carry on a conversation with her during this period, she said no, that he even had trouble signing his name. There were many arguments between mother and son, and sometimes the fight turned from verbal to physical. During one such confrontation, Mrs. Chase was about to call the police, when Richard grabbed the phone's receiver out of her hand and whacked her in the head with it. Somehow she was able to call the police, and with this, Richard ran out the door, jumped over a fence and was gone. When officers arrived, they told Mrs. Chase they'd arrest him if she wanted them to, but she would have to press charges and take out a warrant for his arrest. This was not something Beatrice wanted, so she telephoned the Aquarian Effort, a mental health and substance abuse center. Soon after this, Beatrice decided a trip to southern California to see other family members would do him some good.

And so, Richard Chase was sent to live with his grandmother, Holly Neese, in Los Angeles, and there he worked for his uncle driving a bus for "retarded children." But, like all things, this would not go well either. He wouldn't clean the bus, and he would let it get low on oil. It didn't matter that he was told it wouldn't cost him any money, that all he had to do was take it to a particular station the business used and they would take care of it. Indeed, nothing they said made the slightest difference. When asked about his mental condition and whether Chase acted strangely or abnormally while living with her, Mrs. Neese said yes, and she explained the differences she saw in Richard from the boy she knew when she travelled to Sacramento for visits years earlier. After being fired as the bus driver, she said, he would stay in bed for most of the day and would roam the house at night.

Chase returned to Sacramento for Christmas of 1972. The divorce between Beatrice and Richard Sr. would be finalized the following month, and it's certain they'd heard about the problems Richard was having in L.A. These things, along with Richard's overall condition, no doubt made for a dreary Christmas. On April 22, 1973, while attending a party at a friend's house, Chase attempted to grab the breasts of a girl and was forced to leave. He soon returned, forced his way back inside, and when some of the guys struggled with him, a .22 pistol fell out of his belt. Police were called, and Chase apparently resisted arrest and was forcibly restrained by patrol officers and taken to jail. The next day, he complained of being seriously injured and wanted to sue the police department, but his father again convinced him to let it go. However, this event does seem to be a catalyst in Chase's mind for his full-blown obsession with his physical condition.

In any event, Chase returned to Los Angeles in May of that year, perhaps to a less-than-thrilled grandmother. (Holly Neese said he returned on February 10, 1973, but this date is probably incorrect; and in fact, occasionally conflicting dates exist within the case files, so I have used those dates which most likely are correct.) This stay, however, would not be as long as his previous excursion, and he'd be back home by July of that year. According to Holly Neese, the deterioration, both mental and physical, had intensified during his second trip: "Yes, (it was) the second time he was down here he was terribly dirty ... he came out (of his bedroom) and used my couch in the living room, and he had bread crumbs, and everything just dripped over the couch and all over the floor, and he had papers, newspapers, he'd get newspapers, and I don't know what he wanted to do with them, but he'd have them pulled all apart all over the house." Mrs. Neese would also hear him making a lot of noise at night, and that bothered her. "I would wake up at night," she remembered, "and ... he'd be pounding on things. He was building a speaker for his car ... and he blew the whole side of my electricity out, and half in the living room and in the bathroom ..." She would also hear him talking to himself: "'Richard, you're a good boy aren't you?

Yes, you're a good boy.'" This she heard as many as four or five times.

Chase talked very little while staying with his grandmother. He was paranoid and believed someone was trying to enter the home through a window. Holly Neese also found him standing on his head in the corner of the room. He told her he was trying to get the blood to run back down into his head. He complained his heart was hurting and spoke of pains in his legs. He would also sometimes wrap his head with a towel filled with orange slices, she said. All of this must have been exceedingly disturbing, not just to Holly Neese, but other family members aware of it. And, while Chase attempted to hold down a job at a local paint store, that, too, would end after just ten days. However, he saved enough money with his paint shop wages that he was able to buy a .22-caliber pistol. Knowing his mental instability, Holly Neese was troubled about this from the moment she learned he'd purchased a gun. Later, Chase's grandmother would tell investigators that the family could no longer handle having him around. Chase was put on a plane and returned to Sacramento. The stress on the Chase family, which must have been somewhat alleviated by the absence of Richard, was now back in full force. Indeed, in the months to come, Chase would descend even deeper into the bizarre mental world in which he lived.

When Chase returned, he divided his time between his mother's home on Montclaire and the duplex on Valkyrie Way where his father lived (indeed, after that period when Chase no longer stayed with his father at the duplex, neighbors would report how he would come over, stand in the driveway, and stare blankly at the house). His father, obviously distressed with how his son's life was going, nevertheless, did not see his situation as a mental health issue. Instead, he believed his problems "stemmed from misguided values (and) attitudes." Therefore, he was always telling him to "get a job, shape up, and function normally." These words, of course, had no effect on Richard, and more often than not, the conversations between father and son would end in shouts and disagreement.

Beatrice, who, like her ex-husband, had her own set of problems and issues to deal with, would have the most interaction with Richard and would later tell investigators what Chase's descent into the bizarre was like. As the weeks and months passed, Richard Chase grew more and more preoccupied with his physical condition. According to his mother, he told her "his head was hurting, and his head was changing shape ... He thought there was something wrong with his nervous system ... He thought he was numb (and) that his heart was stopping and he had something wrong with his blood circulation, and he also had a fear of dying." Chase also believed "bones were coming out the back of his head." During this time, Chase began cutting pictures of hearts and other organs out of a *Gray's Anatomy* and taping them to his wall, and it does appear he was driven to understand what was happening to him. One day, the doorbell rang, and when Mrs. Chase answered it, there stood members of the local fire department. Without her knowledge, Richard had called them and said he was a "heart patient and he wanted them to come out and get him. And they came out knocking at the door ... and they brought a stretcher, and they said 'where is the stretcher case,' and he (Richard) came forward and said, 'well, here I am.'"

Of course, what was transpiring had nothing to do with his physical condition. At one point, Chase went to his mother, practically begging for help: "Later on, Richard came up to me, and he said, 'Mom, aren't you going to help me? I'm sick. I want to start tests and everything.'" At this point, Beatrice Chase began contacting doctors. Doctor Donald Ansel, who examined Chase after he was dissatisfied with two previous doctors, said he "had a psychiatric disturbance of major proportion ..." On December 1, 1973, Chase walked into the emergency room at American River Hospital. Telling them he couldn't breathe, he also mentioned he'd "lost his pulmonary vein." He also complained of "cardiac arrest" and that "someone had stolen his pulmonary artery and ... his blood flow had stopped." Chase was also noted to be "tense, nervous, and wild-eyed." Doctor Irwin Lyons wrote in his initial report that the patient was: "a filthy, disheveled, deteriorated, and foul-smelling white male." The doctor's diagnosis was "chronic paranoid schizophrenia (acute) though the possibility (of a) toxic psychosis consequent to ingestion of psychotomimetic drugs cannot be ruled out ..."

Having dealt with the disturbed Richard Chase for the last two days, the medical staff of American River Hospital was about to butt heads with his mother. According to Doctor Lyons' report, Chase was discharged after a confrontation with his mother. In his report of the incident, the doctor noted that Beatrice Chase was "highly aggressive ... hostile ... provocative," quickly adding she was the "so-called schizophrenic mother." Final diagnosis at discharge: "chronic paranoid schizophrenia."

After leaving American River Hospital, Richard Chase had a period of improvement. As he took his medication, he was manageable, and it must have seemed like a godsend to the family. He also was supplied with an oxygen tank, (possibly for panic attacks). Always pathetically thin, Chase succeeded in adding some twenty pounds to his frame, and he was exercising on a regular basis. Beatrice Chase believed this upward swing lasted about two years, but this is disputed by Richard's father. In any event, things would go terribly wrong with Chase, Beatrice said, when he began again to use illegal drugs. No matter the cause, Chase's spiral downward, once begun, would continue without letup, and while the parents couldn't have known it, things were going to become darker in the life of their son.

Just as Chase's grandmother, Holly Neese, heard him talking to himself, so, too, Beatrice would overhear her son carrying on short, but strange conversations: "Oh, shut up," she would hear him spout. When she answered, "What are you, you stop talking to me like that," Chase would reply, "I'm not talking to you." This happened two or three times, she said. Beatrice also told of talking with Richard, when suddenly he'd declare, "I'm not going to do it." She thought he was addressing her, so she said, "Well, now, you're going to do it." But, he quickly responded, "Well, I wasn't talking to you." At least twelve times, Beatrice Chase watched her son take orange slices, wrap them in a towel and place the towel around his head. But, this, like all other attempts he made to relieve whatever stressors were afflicting him, would also fail. As the paranoid delusions increased within his life, so, too, would the accusations he would hurl at his mother and others become more bizarre. It wasn't long before he ordered his mother to stop controlling his mind (this occurred twice), and he accused his sister, Pam, of doing the same thing (one time).

Of course, as the delusions increased, his frustration level would rise, making living with him all but impossible. Over the next couple of years, Beatrice Chase would listen as glass in windows was broken, doors were knocked off their hinges, and holes were kicked in walls. At times, Richard's father would be called, but instead of this having the intended calming effect, it would increase the agitation and anger within him. On one occasion, as Beatrice and Pamela ran from the house in fear while Chase tore up the place, the father, being thus informed, called and attempted to restore order. Chase, however, who was having an emotional meltdown, ripped the phone and its housing completely from the wall. On another occasion, Chase met his father outside, and after heated words were exchanged, they had a fight on the front lawn. Chase had also slapped his mother in the face, and on at least one occasion, knocked her down. There were times when Richard would go on a rampage and break things in the house merely after talking with his father on the phone. Instead of thinking the rage was caused by the discussion with his dad, Beatrice came to believe *that her ex-husband was ordering Richard to do it!* (Italics are mine).

By 1976, Beatrice began to notice other strange things happening with her son; things that spoke of a sadistic nature she'd never seen before: "At this time, my son would actually hurt my dog's foot; he would grab that foot and cut it with his knife." Chase would also squeeze the dog's paws. And, he would squeeze the dog's jaw so hard he nearly broke it, and the animal could not feed for a time. This, as well as the continuing rage within her son, caused Beatrice to get him out of the house, and with the assistance of his father, Richard moved into an apartment on Cannon Street in March of that year. The residence actually was a smaller house, a cottage really, in the rear of the main home, and for a while, Chase kept the place relatively clean, and his main mode of transportation was a bicycle. Being on "general assistance," some of the financial burden Richard was causing had been alleviated. And, it would be here that Richard Chase began drinking the blood of rabbits he'd purchased from an individual in Rio Linda. Mr. Chase, who occasionally came over to play chess with his son, saw the rabbits, and when he asked about them, Chase told him he was eating them. Exceedingly strange, of course, but Mr. Chase was used to strange things coming from his son. He couldn't have imagined what Richard was really doing with them once he was alone.

And then, on the evening of April 25, 1976, Mr. Chase

once again was visiting his son and playing chess. All seemed normal, the rabbits notwithstanding. But, sometime after the father went home (either later that night or the next day), Chase injected himself with rabbit blood. This produced a great deal of vomiting, and when Mr. Chase came to check on his son the next day, Richard could hardly move, he was so ill. Getting him into his car, Mr. Chase drove his son to Community Hospital in north Sacramento. He was immediately admitted, and attending physicians made the following observations: "States he has been 'poisoned by a rabbit he ate' ... gives a bizarre history of eating a rabbit, which had battery acid in its stomach." Diagnosis: "schizophrenia, paranoid type," with an additional comment that Chase was "well-oriented." At that time, a seventy-two-hour hold was placed on the patient.

On the 28th, Chase was transferred to American River Hospital, where, according to the report, "he stayed until May 19, 1976." Admitting physician Doctor Frank Harper said: "Approximately three days ago, drank some blood and attempted to inject rabbit blood into his system ... states he needs to drink blood because his heart is weak." Doctor Harper also noted Chase was "hostile ... but oriented to time, place, and person." While there, Chase complained of "heart weakness," said his "body was falling apart," and refused to participate in an exercise program or attend group therapy. According to staff members, Chase was "almost nonverbal."

Richard Chase was discharged from American River Hospital on May 19. The final notations from

Doctor Michael Buckley paint a dismal picture of his patient: "Uncooperative with treatment throughout the course of his hospitalization. ... Final diagnosis: 'schizophrenia, paranoid type.'" Chase was then transferred to Beverly Manor for extended care, something he wanted nothing to do with. Chase, who was visibly nervous entering the institution, stated, "Food poisoning is why I am here."

However, it wasn't long before the staff noticed a slight improvement in the patient's condition, noting that while he initially was "withdrawn, reclusive, and uncooperative," he "eventually participated more in programs and activities and socialized with other patients and with staff." Even so, Chase still had little patience with being there, and he was under the impression they were treating him for this only. That said, his desire to drink blood had not vanished, and an entry dated June 20, 1976, states the following: "suspected ... has been killing and maiming animals. Two dead birds ... found outside his room with their heads broken off last Wednesday. The housekeeper saw (Chase) outside his room, but could not see what he was doing. ... When he came in, he had blood all over him." When Mr. Chase asked his son about this, Richard told him he'd cut himself shaving. Another orderly found a dead bird in his waste basket. Another time, they found Chase in the bushes, feathers around him and blood on his face.

Despite his thirst for blood and the belief he needed this to stay alive, Chase had another outward spurt of improvement. He played basketball, interacted with staff, and attended more groups. And, this caused his doctors to see at least the possibility of long-term improvement. It was an extremely guarded prognosis, but as Doctor Buckley's report of September 29, 1976, noted, "Thinking much clearer as compared to time of admission. Will discharge to be under care of parents and follow-up physician. Thought disorder improved. Prognosis: Fair. Will continue on same medications. Diagnosis: paranoid schizophrenia. Restorative potential: guarded."

Richard Trenton Chase was coming back to the world.

Chapter Three

Murder Beyond Belief

When Richard Chase walked out the front door of Beverly Manor, he had shown just enough mental improvement to warrant the release. When dealing with these types of situations (and doctors don't like to admit this), releasing a person like Richard Chase back into society is no more than an educated roll of the dice. No one wants to step up and say this, but it's true, nevertheless. After all, as bizarre as his actions were known to be, there was little they could point to that could represent a danger to humans. To be odd, weird, or crazy is not a crime, and under our laws, Chase had rights, as well. It is the great balancing act, where society must make choices — sometimes difficult choices — to protect society, while at the same time, not destroying the constitutionally protected rights of the individual.

After leaving Beverly Manor, Chase's parents, acting as conservators since their son was totally unable to take care of himself, set him up in apartment number 12 at 2934 Watt Avenue. There was little else they could do, and it must have seemed like an endless nightmare. Still, they had him at least functioning in his own place, and as he continued taking his medication, he was, in the words of his mother, "easy to handle." But, what Beatrice Chase didn't like was her son moving about all day "like a zombie." To dislike the effects of what the medicine was doing to keep her son on an even keel was one thing. To take it upon herself to stop his medication was something else altogether. Yet, this is what happened, and his case file contains the following report: Mrs. Chase "took it upon herself to wean (defendant) off all his medications, and by January, 1977, he was no longer taking any drugs." Not only was Chase now off his medication, there were no follow-up visits to outpatient care, nor was he seen regularly by a psychiatrist. Richard Chase, from this time forward, essentially was adrift. This, of course, was a recipe for disaster and was an egregious departure from that which his doctors had prescribed.

Left to his own devices, Chase slept during the day and roamed at night. One particular hangout was the Country Club Lanes Bowling Alley. Here he met other young people, and sometimes these individuals would stay with him in his apartment. He even sublet the apartment for a while, but when he wanted them to leave, he couldn't get them out again. So, Richard Sr. came over and ran them off. For a while, Mr. Chase came over on Sunday mornings, and father and son would go bowling together.

Of course, the illegal use of drugs also became a greater part of his life, and being off his prescribed medication caused his paranoia to flare up once again. During this time, Beatrice had been handling his Social Security payments and paying his rent. (When his father asked him one day why he was getting benefits from Social Security, Chase responded it was because he was "incapacitated to work.") Mrs. Chase said that it was during this period that Richard again started accusing her and his sister of trying to poison him. Although she brought him groceries on a regular basis and was allowed into the apartment (which, according to her, was always filthy), he soon refused to let her inside. Mr. Chase, who also brought food to his son, was barred from entering the apartment, as well. It was just another step in the wrong direction in this terrible situation.

In late 1976 or early 1977, Chase, sporting a "totally shaved head," walked into his doctor's office and spoke to the nurse. He was tired, and he said he hadn't been sleeping well and that he wanted blood. Without an appointment, he was unable to see the doctor, and not receiving any blood, he turned away and left. According to the nurse, Chase would come on other occasions, but, seeing the busy waiting room, would leave without speaking to anyone. Richard Chase was now spiraling out of control, and he was entering a new phase in his mental condition. Heretofore, only small birds and small animals were paying the price to supplement his need for blood. But, he soon would begin killing larger animals. That would be only temporary, though, as the ultimate of sacrifices — the killing of humans — would soon be on the table.

Vampire

In early summer, Richard Chase informed his parents he wanted to "go back east," and he wanted to leave his apartment altogether. Beatrice attempted to get Richard to change his mind, but it was clear his mind was made up. Unable to dissuade him, she helped him clean the place, and Richard Chase moved out of apartment 12. She also gave him some fifteen hundred dollars in Social Security money she'd saved for him. Mr. Chase, who wasn't as concerned as his ex about their son leaving, took Richard to the bus station, where he purchased a ticket for Washington, D.C. When Chase returned, more than two weeks later, he was driving a silver-gray 1966 Ford Ranchero he'd purchased from a John Meyers in Steamboat Springs, Colorado, for eight hundred dollars. Soon after his return, Chase moved back into the Evergreen Apartments on Watt Avenue, this time apartment number 15. It was July 3, 1977.

Chase's 1977 California driver's license

One of his neighbors, Linda Dillon, remembers Richard Chase as being a very weird individual. She later told investigators she'd see him walking around the complex with his mouth hanging open, and sometimes he appeared to be "dragging ... one foot" as he walked. Whenever she passed him in the complex and said hello, he wouldn't respond. She also remembers Chase once entering her apartment "uninvited" and leaving after seeing other people there. Dillon also was "cornered" by Chase one day in the parking lot, where he asked her for a cigarette. When she gave him one, he demanded more, so she turned the pack over to him. Dillon mentioned Chase "had a blank look on his face." She also had noticed Chase carrying two dogs and a cat into his apartment, but she never heard them or ever saw them again. She did, however, see him carrying boxes to and from his place. Around this same time, Chase was seen carrying a shotgun through the complex. This understandably bothered the residents, so the apartment manager asked him to at least wrap the weapon in a blanket if he wanted to carry it around. Chase complied.

That summer of 1977, Chase killed both of the family dogs. (There is no confirmation that the two dogs Dillon saw were the Chase animals, although that possibility does exist.) When confronted by his father, he denied it. Of course, his parents understood he was lying, that the dogs were dead, and this was just one more terrible act from a son who was clearly not getting better. He did later tell his mother (without admitting that he killed them) that the dogs belonged to him and that "I had a right to do what I wanted to." And then, a confrontation between mother and son would leave no doubt as to what he was capable of doing. One afternoon, Beatrice heard knocking on her front door, but, believing it was Richard, she decided not to open it. They'd had a disagreement about something, and she purposely was avoiding him. The next thing she heard was a loud bang. Opening the door, she saw Richard holding her dead cat by the tail. The bullet, which probably entered the head, splattered blood and tissue on her front porch, and as she stared at him, Richard wiped the cat's blood on the back of his neck. When she told Richard Sr. what their son had done, she oddly left out the part about Chase smearing the blood on his neck.

On August 3, Richard Chase was sitting in the hot sun along a rocky area of Pyramid Lake, Nevada, some two hundred miles from Sacramento. He was completely naked and was covered in blood. He wasn't in a hurry, just sitting there. Approximately one-half to three-quarters of a mile away (and across the lake) sat his Ford Ranchero. Inside the vehicle were two rifles, a .22 caliber and a Marlin .30-30 lever-action. Both weapons had blood on them, as did most of the inside of the vehicle. There was a white bucket, too, which contained blood and a liver. Earlier that morning, Chase had gotten the truck stuck in the sand. Perhaps, without Chase knowing it, a Mr. Carman Tobey Sr. had watched him leave the Ranchero with a dog, heading, as he said, "to the Pinnacles area." Mr. Tobey soon telephoned the authorities. According to the report, Bureau of Indian

Affairs officers Charles O'Brien, Manuel Sabori, and Leland Johnson, along with Tribal officers Leroy Phoenix and Edward Crutcher responded to the call.

"At this time," Officer O'Brien wrote in his report, "I started to scan the area with field glasses, and as I looked to the south, I saw a white male subject squatting in the sand, watching us. He was approximately one-half to three-quarters of a mile away from us. He was completely nude. Officers Johnson and Sabori started after him on foot. Subject then started running towards the lake, with officers in foot pursuit. Tribal officers Phoenix and Crutcher started out to head subject off; the officers were equipped with a four-wheel-drive vehicle." Within minutes, Chase was apprehended. Chase had no trouble letting the officers know his correct name, age, and address. But, when asked about the blood covering him and in his truck, he sounded confused and like he was giving evasive answers: "I asked Mr. Chase where all the blood on his face came from. He told me that the blood was seeping from his skin. I asked some further questions, which he would not answer. I then asked him again about the blood on his face and body. He told me then that he had shot a deer. I asked him where and when, and he told me in Colorado in May." The dog accompanying Chase that morning was now missing, and when questioned about it, he said he didn't know where the dog was. The investigators also noticed he was wearing a knife sheath, but the knife was missing.

After a brief struggle, Chase was arrested and held while the blood and liver found in the Ranchero were

Vampire

tested. "We arrived at the ranger station ..." O'Brien wrote in his report, "I placed a call to the U.S. Attorney in Reno, and informed him of the situation. I was told by U.S. Deputy Attorney Ray Pike to place him under arrest for violation of U.S.C. 18, Section 922, G & H. Mr. Chase was then placed under arrest and given his Miranda warning and then transported and booked into the Washoe County jail." When the lab reports came back that the blood and liver were from an animal, Chase was released.

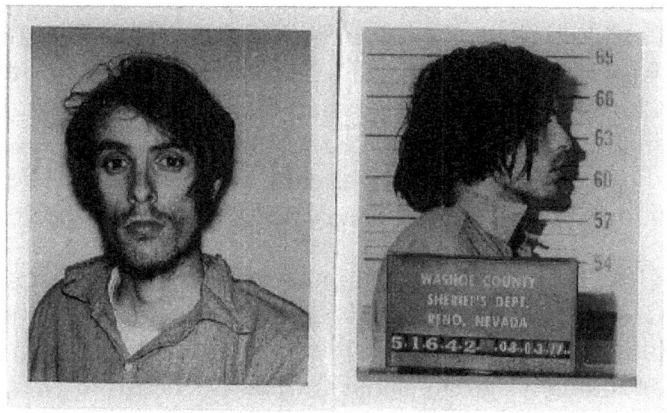

Pyramid Lake arrest

The Ranchero, however, was not released due to a problem with the registration. When Chase called his mother, he lied about the real problem, telling her it was all a big mix-up, as he'd really just killed some rabbits, had gotten blood all over himself, and was mistakenly arrested. Mr. Chase drove to Sparks, Nevada, to pick up his son, and Richard gave him the same story. This, of course, is a perfect illustration of how he was able to conceal his true intentions. Yes, his actions were bizarre and spoke of severe mental problems, as diagnosed by the medical professionals. But, it was his ability to think and plot and deceive that would come back to haunt him after society captured him. In any event, Chase traveled back to Sparks, Nevada, to obtain the release of his car. Not only did he have to prove actual ownership (having purchased the vehicle from Mr. Meyers, the original owner), but he had the snag of having expired Florida license tags, as well. Ms. Macia Luis, of the Washoe County Sheriff's Department, dealt with Chase several times during this period. Although she reported Chase looked "raunchy" every time he showed up, he always was calm and courteous. After numerous attempts, Chase was given his Ranchero.

That fall (and only months before the Ambrose Griffin murder), Chase's desire to drink the blood of animals increased significantly, and he began obtaining dogs to satisfy what he believed were his needs. The following is a brief record from the case file of Richard Chase's activities involving the purchasing and stealing of dogs: "On October 1, 1977, Chase bought a dog from the SPCA for fifteen dollars and ninety cents. On October 10, 1977, he bought another dog from the SPCA for the same price."

In October or November, Chase went to the home of Alane Maier to purchase a dog. The advertised price was twenty-five dollars, but Chase tried to talk them down to twenty-three dollars, to no avail, and grumbled about having to spend the extra two bucks. Alane Maier later told investigators that Chase acted normal and that the dog did not want to go with him. The dog's tags later were recovered in his apartment. In mid-November, Chase again responded to an ad for Labrador puppies, ten dollars apiece. The seller, a Mr. Daniel Owens, said he returned home at 4:00 p.m. and found Chase staring over his back fence. Chase then introduced himself as a breeder and asked if he could get a two-for-one price. Owens agreed, and Chase then "took two, paying no attention to sex."

Also in mid-November, Chase grabbed a dog belonging to the Sundseth family (very close to Chase's apartment), and wasn't content with simply killing and mutilating the dog. When the Sundseths placed an ad in the newspaper, Chase called and taunted them, giving details that only the person having the dog would know. This unnerved the daughter so badly she handed the phone to her father, but Chase immediately hung up. The Sundseths said the man sounded somewhat incoherent and may have been high on drugs. The dog's tag and collar were later found in his residence. About this same time, Chase attempted to steal a Saint Bernard from the Hoey residence on Morse Avenue, but was unsuccessful. (Joann Hoey's neighbor informed her of this). When Chase came by a second time, Joann Hoey had just pulled away from her house, but she noticed Chase, whom she later identified in court, heading up her driveway. She quickly drove back and asked him what he wanted. Without saying a word, the strange man left. The Hoeys' Saint Bernard would not become a victim of Richard Trenton Chase. He would later admit taking the other dogs back to his apartment and hanging them. Chase would then drink their blood and also was "eating dog viscera, raw."

On December 2, 1977, Richard Chase entered Big 5 Sporting Goods and purchased a Stoeger Arms, Luger-style .22-caliber pistol. There was a waiting period, so Chase could not pick up the gun for two weeks. When asked whether he was "a mental patient or on leave of absence from any mental hospital or has he ever been adjudicated by a court to be a danger to others as a result of a mental disorder or mental illness," Chase said no. He must have exhausted his funds purchasing the weapon (he paid sixty-nine dollars and ninety-nine cents cash), as he asked his mother to buy him a holster. She refused. Linda Dillon, who would soon be leaving the complex, states she heard shooting inside Chase's apartment on at least two occasions. Chase later confirmed this, saying he was "shooting at voices heard in apartment," and detectives would later find the holes backing up his story.

On the 16th of December, as if in preparation for what was to come, he cleaned himself up by cutting his hair, trimming his beard, and even "talked of getting a job." Two days later, he went by the sporting goods store and picked up the pistol. He also purchased a fifty-round box of ammunition. On December 22 and 23, he purchased copies of *The Sacramento Bee*, and some of these pages he would keep from the "Out and About" section with an article on singles and dating. Chase also held onto the ads offering free dogs, and some of these were circled. Because he'd mentioned to his mother he wanted a coat, his father picked him up a few days before Christmas and drove him to Weinstock's, a Sacramento-based department store. Here Mr. Chase purchased an orange down parka Richard liked. Mr. Chase soon would be telling investigators how Richard appeared fine on that day, that "he seemed all right, but after the purchase was anxious to leave." The report also noted that over the next month, Richard Sr. spoke to his son several times, and "on these occasions, Chase said nothing bizarre or abnormal, and did not complain about his blood."

Interestingly, the closer Chase approached his time of committing murder, the better he became in his physical appearance and demeanor. Both his parents noticed this, as did his grandmother, Holly Neese, who'd come to Sacramento for the holidays. There was no actual internal improvement, but the outer Richard Chase was transforming into a more palatable person to be around. And yet, because of his prior egregious actions with the family (killing the cat, for example), Richard was not allowed to come over for Christmas. Despite his practically begging them to be a part of the family gathering, Beatrice would not allow it. During an interview with the assistant district attorney, Beatrice Chase and her mother, Holly Neese, spoke of this incident: "In the last year," Neese explained, "she would not allow Rick on the place at all. Every time he would knock on the door, she would run him off. I don't think this was right at all, but she (said) she wouldn't let him come down to Christmas dinner, and he was very upset about it." Beatrice immediately spoke up, saying, "I have an explanation for that. I felt awful about not inviting him down at Christmas, but I did invite him to go out with me. I took all his gifts and lots of good things up there for him to his apartment, but it wasn't like being with the people that he wanted and loved, (I don't know, I hope that he loves). Anyway, my daughter is deathly afraid of him after the cat episode, and after the dog (episode) she said, 'mom, I don't want him around anymore.'" "He just called and called," Neese interjected, "and wanted to come down at Christmas." When Beatrice and her mother visited Chase at his apartment, he seemed surprised about the presents, exclaiming, "all of these for me?" Later, when the two returned and took him to dinner, Chase was looking normal, and according to them, was "dressed in new clothes (and) looked good."

The day after Christmas, Chase purchased an additional box of ammunition. In little more than a day, he'd fire at the Phares residence. And, by the 29th, he would kill Ambrose Griffin as he was retrieving the last bag of groceries, and authorities would not know what to make of this motiveless crime. On January 5, 1978, Chase picked up a copy of *The Sacramento Bee* and would keep (as a trophy) the editorial about the killing of Ambrose Griffin. Later, when all of this was discovered, it would be noted that his actions did, in fact, reflect "awareness of societal condemnation." The next day, Chase picked up that day's edition, keeping the section highlighting a knife murder on the first page of section two.

Although murder was already in his mind, arson was rising in Chase, as well. On January 16, Chase started a fire in a garage in the 3000 block of Watt Avenue. Lighting some newspapers sitting on a shelf, the fire was discovered quickly and put out. Apparently, he believed the people in the neighborhood were spying on him, and he wanted to drive them away. Oddly, he knocked on the door of this residence to make sure no one would die. A few days later, Chase was speaking to his mother and mentioned he wanted to go rock hunting, and so on Saturday, January 21, Mr. Chase picked him up, and the two spent time together hiking and rock hunting. Richard Sr. said his son "did not act bizarre, said nothing unusual, no complaints about health, no arguments," and that they "got along well together." A little over twelve hours later (around 1:00 a.m. on the 22nd), Chase broke a window at 3040 Watt Avenue, crawled inside, and set fire to the drapes of the Nelson residence. Again, as Chase would later tell investigators, he checked to see if anyone was home. The fire department was called quickly, and they put out a fire that had spread to a speaker cabinet and the carpet.

In the early evening of the 22nd, Chase departed from the normal protocol and visited his mother at her house. Grandmother Neese was still visiting, and both women believed Richard looked fine and was doing well. Holly Neese even gave her grandson ten dollars before he left. As Chase was leaving, he asked Holly Neese about her dog and how it was doing!

The two would never have believed what he'd been up to, or what was about to unfold within the quiet neighborhoods of east Sacramento.

When Chase awoke on the morning of January 23, 1978, something had changed within him. He may not have realized it, but he was about to enter a new realm of murder that was unlike anything he had participated in previously. True, he had murdered Ambrose Griffin in cold blood as the man went about his business in his own front yard. But, it was almost a sanitized killing compared to what he was about to do. When he shot Mr. Griffin, he already was headed away from the scene by the time the still-living body fell to the ground. The killing of Ambrose was heartless and sociopathic, and its effect on Mr. Griffin and his family was immediate and everlasting. But, what was about to occur today was far more than just murder; it was diabolical in the truest sense of the word. For in a matter of hours, an evil entity would be unleashed, and the acts committed would shock not just a community, but hardened investigators, as well.

Leaving his apartment on Watt Avenue, Chase headed east on foot, walking the very short distance of several blocks to Burnece Street. He was wearing a blue jacket and had his loaded Luger-style, semi-automatic .22 and a pair of rubber gloves. When he came to 2909 Burnece, there was no car in the driveway, so Chase went around to the back of the house and tried to force open the door. Jeanne Layton, who was watching television, heard a noise in the rear of the house and found Chase on her back porch. It was between 9:00 and 10:00 a.m. Chase saw her through the window and blurted out, "Excuse me," and Ms. Layton wasted no time calling the police. Chase, who sat on her porch for the next few minutes, contemplated killing her and how he could get into her house, according to investigators. But, if this is a fact, he quickly abandoned the idea and left. From there, he walked north (oddly, staying on Burnece, even though he understood the police had been called) and decided to enter the Edwards residence at 2929 Burnece. This time, the house was empty, but the owners were on their way home not long after Chase began his burglary. Chase entered through a rear window, and once inside, he went through drawers and boxes. Within minutes, Chase had sixteen dollars in his hands, and after finding the cash, he began loading a bag with other valuables. Unlike any normal burglar, however, Chase took the time to urinate in a drawer filled with clothing and defecated on a child's bed. Interestingly, the Edwards and the Layton homes were the only two houses on the block that morning that didn't have cars in the driveway.

In any event, before Chase could exit the house, the owners returned, and he fled out the back window and jumped over a fence. But, this didn't stop Mr. Edwards from pursuing him. As the two men ran through the neighborhood, Edwards kept yelling for him to stop. (This is a very human reaction, but who would listen to such a request?) And, at one point, Chase yelled back, "I'm only taking a shortcut." Chase did finally give Edwards the slip, but only temporarily, as Edwards returned home, got into his car, and spotted Chase on Watt Avenue. Soon, however, Richard Chase was back inside his apartment, but only long enough to change his jacket, as he had more things to do that day.

At approximately 11:45 a.m., Richard Chase made his way to the parking lot of the Pantry Market, located in the Town and Country Village. He was wearing his new orange parka, he was extremely dirty, with some type of crusty substance around his mouth, and he certainly stood out to others as being abnormal. Within minutes of Chase arriving at the Pantry Market, a high school friend of his, Nancy Westfall (now Holden), parked her car and entered the store. No sooner had she started her shopping than she heard a man's voice calling out her name. As she turned around, he said, "Weren't you on Curt's motorcycle when he was killed?" Nancy said "no" and asked him who he was. He then identified himself as "Rick," and she said, "You're Rick Chase," and Chase said, "You're Nancy Westfall." Chase then nodded and turned away.

Although Chase broke off the conversation, within minutes he was back wanting to talk with her. "I came down the aisle," Nancy told detectives, "and I could see I wasn't going to avoid him, so I walked up and said, 'What have you been up to, Rick?' And he said, 'Where are you going?' And I gestured toward the cash register. And he said, 'To the bank?' and I said, 'yes.' And he said, 'What, do you have to write a check or something?' and I said, 'no, I do it for work.'" Nancy Holden, who'd later remark how filthy Chase was (she immediately noticed the yellowish crust encircling his mouth), had only one thing on her mind — getting away from this very weird person. As she paid for her items, Chase stood behind her with only an orange drink to purchase. As soon as Holden finished checking out, she hurried towards the door. Chase, seeing she was heading out to the parking lot, called out, "wait ... hey wait," but Nancy Holden had no intention of waiting. As she backed out of the space, Chase caught up with her and attempted to grab the passenger door handle, but missed it by a foot as she sped out of the lot. Driving away, she looked in her rearview mirror and, for a second, watched as Chase just stood there looking in her direction, before turning and walking away, Holden believed, to the rear of the Pantry Market. Just happy to be away from him, Holden would not give the encounter another thought until the upcoming horrific events began to rattle this quiet community.

On the morning of January 23, 1978, Teresa Wallin, twenty-two, walked out her back door at the home where she and her husband lived at 2630 Tioga Way. She walked through her backyard, continued out the back gate, and in little over a minute entered the Pantry Market. The checker, who knew Wallin, said she was in the store between 10:30 a.m. and noon and that she cashed a check while there. A pretty girl, Teresa had been married to David Wallin for almost three years and was three months' pregnant. Upon leaving the store, she walked straight home. Her husband, employed as a truck driver at National Linen, had left about 6:30 that morning while she was still asleep. Teresa, a state worker, had the day off. David was, in fact, training another driver that morning, as he soon would be leaving for another job. On this day, he'd be traveling from Sacramento to Lake Tahoe, showing Jim Cody everything he'd need to know to get the job done.

Richard Chase, who watched Nancy Holden drive away from the Pantry Market, turned and began walking towards Tioga Way, which sits directly behind the grocery store. He passed through a small park located between the market and Tioga (and several houses down from the Wallin residence) and immediately turned left and walked across the front porch of Richard and Sheila Eastlick at 2710 Tioga Way. Richard Eastlick, who'd been watching television in his living room, immediately got up and saw a thin, white male wearing an "orange ski jacket" heading towards Fulton Avenue. Two doors down (towards Fulton Avenue) sat the Wallin home. Richard Eastlick's brother, Harry, and his wife, Patricia, live at 2731 Tioga Way. That morning, Patricia, said she saw a man in an orange jacket walk across her brother-in-law's porch between 11:30 a.m. and 12:00 p.m., and walk across the next porch, as well. And, that's when he passed out of sight.

Vampire

Police aerial photo

It was a quiet day. Teresa Wallin was busy cleaning, and it seems certain that whatever thoughts were flowing through her mind at that moment would have been normal; the thought of her life ending would never have entered her mind. But, the front door had been left unlocked, and a strange man bent on murder even then was coming closer to her home. When the front door flew open, Richard Chase, wasting no time, pulled out the .22-caliber pistol and aimed it at the startled young woman, who was carrying a white plastic garbage bag out of the house. Seeing the weapon, Teresa had time to throw her right arm up in a vain attempt to protect her head. Chase fired once, the bullet passing through Wallin's hand near the wrist and grazing her head. The next shot slammed into her cheek, breaking her jaw. Chase fired a third time, and this last bullet pierced her brain, rendering her unconscious and dying. Chase would later tell detectives that he "just wanted to kill her, it could have been anybody," and, "she tried to avoid the shots." Richard Eastlick would tell investigators he heard what he thought were "three or four shots coming from the south of his residence."

The home of David and Teresa Wallin

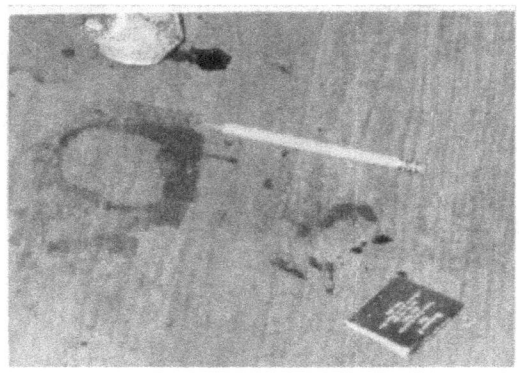

Blood marks and the yogurt cup Chase used to drink Teresa Wallin's blood

Vampire

With Wallin not yet dead and lying on the living room floor, Chase put on rubber gloves and dragged his victim to a rear bedroom. Here he began his diabolical work. Leaving her on the floor, Chase pulled her sweater and bra above her breasts and pulled her pants and panties down to her ankles. He took her left leg and angled it to the right and bent it, exposing her pubic region. Taking a knife from the kitchen, Chase began to mutilate the young wife and mother-to-be. According to court records, Richard Chase "attacked specific organs ... pancreas cut in half ... spleen completely cut out of body ... stomach cut ... liver cut ... part of large and small intestines pulled out of the way and connecting tissue damaged, but no incidental cutting of intestine ... membrane between intestines and kidney penetrated (no way to get to kidneys through abdomen from front without doing this). Both kidneys cut out of their proper positions, one nearly cut in half ... diaghram (sic) ... had hole in it ... one kidney found in chest ... portion of lower left lung completely sawed off ... stabs into heart ... opinion of pathologist — this was not random, but was attacks on specific ... some of this was done before she was dead." While doing this, Chase used an empty yogurt cup and was able to fill it with blood, and then drank from the cup. Investigators also found blood ringlets on the floor next to her body, as if made by a bucket. And it would not be the last time detectives would see such things.

Chase also stabbed Teresa Wallin through the left breast, "once superficially, once through the nipple, and on through to the lung, thrusting knife three times through wound." Chase placed dried dog feces that he'd retrieved from the backyard in her mouth. After killing and mutilating his victim, Chase, still wearing the rubber gloves, went into the bathroom and washed up. He then took the knife and wiped it with a scarf before washing it off and laying it underneath other dishes in the dish rack. Chase left through the back door and exited the property through the back gate. Richard Chase would later tell a psychiatrist that he "went home (and) watched television (and) waited for the paper to come."

David Wallin had spent eight hours training his replacement. After the last run of the day had been made, the two men clocked out around 5:00 p.m., and Jim Cody followed Wallin over to Slick Willies Bar at Fulton and Cottage. After splitting two pitchers of beer, the two men called it a night, and David Wallin got into his car for the short drive home. As Wallin put the key into the front door, he could not have known how drastically his life was about to change. Later, he would tell detectives that while he turned the key, he didn't know if the door was actually locked. Just before entering, David flipped on the porch light to give him some light, as the house was dark. In any event, as he stepped into his home, he discovered that not only was the house dark, but the stereo was playing. From the illumination of the porch light, he immediately noticed garbage strewn all about the room. He called out to Teresa, but received no answer, and their German shepherd, Brutus, came up to him and was acting strangely. He also spotted what he thought was a circular patch of oil on the floor and followed additional "spots" leading to the master bedroom. Rounding the corner, he was met with the lifeless and mutilated body of his wife, telling investigators he saw "a large wound in her stomach, her tongue hanging out, and her eyes open." The nipple on her left breast had also been cut off. Overwhelmed with the horror of the sight, David Wallin said he only looked at her for just a second before getting out of the room.

Although Wallin started screaming and didn't know what to do, he managed to call his father, and his brother, John, answered the phone. Being so upset, he doesn't remember what he said to his brother, but in an instant, his father was on the phone telling his son he'd be right over. No doubt in panic-mode, David Wallin then rushed out of the house and went next door to his neighbor's home, saying, "My wife is dead." The neighbors, of course, did everything they could to comfort him, and they made the call to the sheriff's office. After a few minutes, David walked outside to see if his parents had arrived, and as they hadn't, he went back inside his neighbor's home. Several minutes later, he again went outside, glanced over at his house, and this time he saw his father's car, but it was empty. With this, Wallin ran towards his home, hoping to reach his dad before he went into the bedroom where Teresa was lying. Bursting through the front door, he found his parents in the kitchen and learned they'd already seen the body of their daughter-in-law.

Within minutes of this, patrol officers Gary Flanagan and Tom Savage responded to the scene. As they pulled up to the house, they noticed the front door was open and several people were standing in the living room. When David saw the patrol car, he and his parents walked onto the porch. And, as the officers approached them, David Wallin said, "You've got a murder on your hands, boys. My wife's in the bedroom, she's been murdered." While Officer Flanagan waited on the porch with the distraught Wallin family, Patrolman Savage went in to see Teresa Wallin (later, Savage would tell reporters about the nightmares he'd experienced after the Wallin murder). Although Savage knew from looking at her she was dead, he checked her carotid artery for a pulse, but found none. A quick shining of light into her eyes revealed unresponsive pupils, as well. After Savage rejoined the group on the porch, Flanagan viewed the body of Teresa Wallin, and he, too, checked her carotid artery and did the pupil test, all with the same results. At this time, the officers secured the scene and contacted the dispatcher to send detectives from homicide, as well as the coroner. Although police did an initial interview with the Wallins at the scene, a more extensive questioning would occur several days later.

As can be expected with any murder, Tioga Way soon was a sea of police. Heading up the investigation was Lieutenant Ray Biondi, an experienced investigator and all-around good cop, who was well-respected by those who knew him. On the evening of the murder of Teresa Wallin, rookie detectives Bill Roberts and Wayne Irey came on the scene, and as Roberts was talking with his commander, Biondi told him, "We need to hurry up and catch the sick son of a bitch who did this." It was clear to Biondi that whoever had done it was likely to do it again, and that meant they were in a race against time.

On January 26, investigators questioned David Wallin about his and Teresa's recent activity, and it wasn't long before police not only knew his story was credible, but learned how normal the last several days had been for the young couple. Beginning with Friday evening and ending on the morning of the murder, David Wallin related the activities and interactions he had with Teresa and others. That Friday evening the couple went to Senor Pepe's on Fulton Avenue, and then later played cards with friends until 3:00 in the morning. Saturday consisted of dinner at home and watching television all evening. On Sunday, the couple went bowling in the morning, and then to David's parents' home, where they had breakfast and David played basketball with his brother. David and Teresa then visited another couple before returning home. When David awoke Monday morning, he left for work before his wife had awakened.

The day after the murder of Teresa Wallin, Richard Chase purchased a copy of *The Sacramento Bee*. Of course, Chase loved reading about the murders he'd committed, and he would keep this newspaper and add it to those papers he kept pertaining to the Ambrose Griffin killing. But, it wouldn't be all about reading, and on that day, Chase would start canvassing the neighborhoods close to his residence for more individuals to murder. He would do so under the guise of wanting old magazines, and his strange actions would be noticed by others. Chase's thirst for blood had only just begun.

Between 10:00 and 10:30 a.m. on the 24th, Chase walked up to the front door of Lawrence and Betty Lawman at 3216 Sunview Avenue. While Chase was standing at the door, he was checking out the Pontiac in the driveway. When Mr. Lawman asked him what he wanted, Chase said old magazines. Lawman said he didn't have any, and Chase left. He was next spotted at 1:00 p.m. at 2412 Brentwood (both Brentwood and Sunview are very close to Merrywood) and asked for magazines, but was turned away. "There are," the report continues, "possible sightings of him the same day at the Carson residence (at) 2405 Park Estates Drive and the Hall residence, 2419 Meadowbrook," (both streets intersect with Merrywood). Although it's without question that Richard Chase was looking for more people to kill, he called his mother later that evening (she wasn't home, so he spoke to his grandmother) to ask her if she wanted to go on a picnic. According to Holly Neese, her grandson "seemed in good spirits."

Not wanting to leave the area he'd been casing, Chase returned to the neighborhood and was observed on the 25th around 10:15 a.m. at the Heise residence at 3133 Pennland, which runs parallel to Merrywood and only one block north. Here, he again asked for old magazines, but did not receive any. Not having any luck finding humans to kill, Chase revisited the Owens place, where he'd purchased two puppies in November. As Chase knew Mr. Owens' schedule (he was at work), he felt no trepidation for what he was about to do. Chase was able to get to one of the Labradors, and he killed it through a couple shots to its head. He then cut open the dog's stomach and removed the kidneys. Without question, he drank some of the dog's blood. That night, Chase called his mother, and this time, she was home. During the conversation, he spoke of "rockets, spacecraft, (and) joked about little green men." Beatrice Chase also mentioned she and Richard had a "jolly conversation."

While Chase was looking for more victims, the police were working long hours knocking on doors and following up every available lead. In police work, it's routine to consider anyone a "suspect" in a homicide investigation, but most people who know the victim are ruled out very quickly. One individual, an ex-girlfriend of David Wallin, did raise the eyebrows of the authorities for a moment, but this, too, would soon be a dead end. And, in fact, while there were other homicides to solve in Sacramento and the Sheriff's Department had instituted a task force to catch an individual known as the East Area Rapist (EAR) who had racked up thirty-eight rapes in two years, nothing could compare with the diabolical ferocity of the murder of Teresa Wallin. As Lieutenant Ray Biondi would later say, "Never in the history of the Sacramento County Sheriff's Department had anyone reported a scene like that on Tioga Way." To say that the law enforcement community was overtaxed at this time would be an understatement.

On January 26, Chase had migrated to Merrywood

Drive. As mentioned earlier, all of his crimes, violent and otherwise, were committed in a geographically small area, stretching only short distances to the north, east, south, or west of his apartment on Watt Avenue. On this day, Chase would stop at the Scott residence at 2407 Merrywood, and he spoke to Mrs. Scott, asking for magazines. Mrs. Scott had some difficulty hearing him, so she partially opened the door and Chase mumbled something about "magazines and newspapers." Like the others, she told him no. Chase next stopped at the Klimek home at 2837 Merrywood around 11:00 a.m. Knocking on the door, Ms. Klimek looked through the peephole and asked, "Who's there?" But, the visitor didn't answer. She then asked what he wanted; he said magazines, but she said no. Chase sat on her porch for a few minutes before leaving. Police are convinced the reason Chase sat down was that he was pondering the possibilities of killing her. Not being legally insane, they believed Chase weighed the pros and cons of launching an attack on Ms. Klimek. In any event, he decided to leave and was soon seen by others in the neighborhood, as well. Some report him as already wearing gloves (a slight departure from the Wallin murder, where he put the gloves on after killing his victim), and that he was, true to form, acting oddly.

When he stopped at the Sites residence (also on Merrywood), he did not knock on the door, as if he was casing it. Their dog, however, quickly became aware of his presence and started barking. After looking into a window, he walked away. Chase then walked across the street and stared at the house "for one minute, then walked away fast." Ms. Sites, who later positively identified Richard Chase at his trial, said he was wearing gloves at this time. It is unknown how long Chase searched for a victim or victims on that day, but it's certain he came up empty-handed. It's also unknown whether Chase predetermined a return trip to Merrywood Drive the following day, but of all the streets in the area he could visit in the morning, he would return to Merrywood, and he would find what he was looking for.

As David Wallin said his public good-byes to his wife and all who knew and loved her grieved with him, Detective Ken Baker, having been pulled off the burglary detail, watched with other officers for any unusual persons attending her funeral. Photographs were taken and license numbers were recorded, just in case the killer might show up. It was a long shot, but it's happened before, and the police wanted to be ready for him.

Chapter Four

When Murder is Random

Was it an unconscious compulsion that drove Richard Chase to return to Merrywood Drive that morning of the 27th? All we know for a certainty is that the killer was going back to this quiet and unassuming street to pick up where he'd left off a day earlier. Leaving the Evergreen Apartments, Chase drove south along Watt, crossing first over Marconi Avenue and then crossing over El Camino Avenue, before turning into the parking lot of the Country Club Center. From here, it was but a matter of minutes before he entered Merrywood Drive on foot, which dead-ends at the parking lot of Country Club Center. Later, witnesses would tell authorities they saw Chase's vehicle parked at the center between 10:00 a.m. and noon.

The Miroth residence at 3207 Merrywood Drive sits on the north side of the block and is the third house from the dead end, which separates the street from the parking lot of Country Club Center. Described later as a "modest ranch house," the home looks larger in photographs, but strangely small when viewing it from the street. The home at that time was owned by Evelyn Miroth, thirty-six, and she lived there with her two sons, thirteen-year-old Vernon (named after his father), and Jason, six. Divorced, Evelyn had both a steady boyfriend and a male friend by the name of Daniel Meredith who was fifty. It would be Daniel Meredith's misfortune to be visiting the Miroth family on this particular morning.

The home of Evelyn Miroth

Evelyn Miroth and her nephew, David Ferreira

Jason Miroth

Evelyn Miroth did not work, but she did spend time babysitting her young nephew, twenty-two-month-old David Michael Ferreira. At approximately 7:00 a.m., Karen Ferreira dropped her son off at her sister-in-law's house, in what should have been a routine Friday. Sometime that morning, Evelyn Miroth mowed her yard (presumably, while the infant slept) and subsequently left the garage door open. There was, in fact, a hub of activity that morning at the Miroth residence, with the early morning visit of her friend Daniel Meredith. At approximately 8:30 a.m., Neone Grangaard, who lived at 3212 Merrywood Drive (which sits almost directly across the street from the Miroth residence), called Evelyn to ask her if Jason could accompany her and her two daughters to the mountains to play in the snow. Evelyn said yes. At 9:05, Evelyn called her friend, asking if they could wait until about 10:00, giving her time to purchase snow shoes for Jason. Grangaard readily agreed.

At 9:30, Grangaard noticed Daniel Meredith's bright red station wagon in Miroth's driveway. Twenty-five minutes later, she watched Mr. Meredith get back into his car and drive away. By 10:30, she noticed his station wagon was back, but Meredith had already gone back inside the house. Of course, 10:00 o'clock came and went, and there was no sign of Jason walking across the street to join the Grangaard family for the outing. And, by the time Daniel Meredith reentered the house, her phone calls were not being answered.

It is important to note here that while authorities know exactly what Richard Chase did to the Miroth family and their visitor, Daniel Meredith, on that day, the sequence of events is open to question. Court records state succinctly, "Between 10:00 a.m. and 11:15 a.m., Chase entered the Miroth residence and killed everyone inside." Indeed, it is very likely that by the time Meredith walked back into the house they were already dead (as he stepped in blood while entering), and he, too, was immediately killed. The following is not only the events of that day as described in the police reports, but most likely the order in which they happened.

As Richard Chase left the parking lot of the Country Club Center (where he left his Ranchero parked oddly, not in a usual parking space, but near a "concrete enclosed planter"), he was wearing the new orange jacket and carrying the .22-caliber Luger pistol. In his pocket were also rubber gloves, and it was a mere hundred feet as he strolled down Merrywood before he noticed the open garage door at 3207. He had been on this street a day earlier, and he'd now returned. There was only one car in the garage, which was a good sign to Chase, who apparently avoided houses that might have numerous adults in the house at the same time. Probably entering through an unlocked door (there was no sign of forced entry), it was less than thirty seconds before he encountered Evelyn Miroth in the hallway and startled her. As he no doubt had slipped on the gloves in the garage and cocked the pistol, he was ready to murder the moment he encountered anyone. Coming face-to-face with Miroth, he fired once and sent a bullet into her brain, rendering her unconscious and heading towards death. Jason, who had gone to the store with Daniel Meredith to purchase the shoes, was only momentarily spared the carnage taking place at his home.

It is unknown when little David Ferreira was murdered, but he was killed while in his crib with a shot that entered the right side of his head, passing through it, and piercing the pillow case but not penetrating the pillow. There were bloody footprints around the crib, and some brain matter belonging to the toddler was found in the bathtub. This brain matter was released by Chase, having taken the child into the bathroom, where he dangled him over the tub and gouged out a section of the back of the skull with a knife. This was done, authorities believe, so that Chase could more easily drink the baby's blood. Little David Ferreira would also sustain cutting wounds to his anus, and eventually (at Chase's apartment) he would be decapitated. Miroth's older son, Vernon, was at school at the time of the murders, and her daughter, Lori, was living with her father, Evelyn's ex-husband, Vernon Miroth. Mr. Miroth would arrive at his ex-wife's residence at about the same time sheriff's deputies and homicide investigators were racing to the scene. His reason for being there was to pick up Vernon Jr., who hadn't arrived home from school.

At some point, Richard Chase was interrupted by the arrival of Daniel Meredith and Jason. Meeting them in the front room, Chase fired the pistol at Meredith's head. Hitting his mark, the bullet passed through his head and burrowed into the wall. Chase then shot at Jason, hitting him in the back of the neck, followed by another shot to the boy's head. Although certainly already dead, Chase fired another bullet into Meredith's skull. Later, he would explain to investigators that: "He had nightmares about them and feels that they could come back from the dead, but he has not seen or heard them." When the bodies were found, Jason was wearing his new snow shoes, purchased less than an hour before his death. Daniel Meredith, who was being treated for a benign brain tumor, had met Evelyn Miroth through his sister, Rosemary Wanta.

Once Chase had the privacy and the time to desecrate the body of Evelyn Miroth, he wasted no time doing so. Dragging her from the hallway and into the bathroom, Chase stripped her of all her clothes. He also removed some or most of his clothes. His bloody socks were later found in the residence. What follows is a detailed report of the injuries to Evelyn Miroth. It is not known if all the mutilation happened in one area of the house only, but part did occur in the bathroom (having sex with her dead body, for example), where for a time he pitched her body over the tub (on her stomach), leaving her halfway in the tub and halfway out. She was later pulled into her bedroom, where some of the cutting would be easier for Chase to perform (as in cutting around her eye) after placing her on the edge of the bed.

Mrs. Miroth was mutilated as follows:

Cross shaped cut to abdomen — nine-inch horizontal, five-inch vertical

Some edges smooth, some show jagged sawing — not a wild slash

Liver cut four times

Connecting tissue for membranes holding small intestines was cut

Several loops of small intestines lay outside wound, but small intestine not cut

Stomach was partially pulled out of wound

Membranes behind the intestines was cut (yet intestines not cut)

Cut through anus, up into rectum, two cuts in rectal wall, six puncture marks uterus.

(Knife thrust back and forth in wound.)

(NOTE: All above wounds very close to time of death, did not contribute to death).

Eight cuts to neck, superficial, clearly post mortem, ranging from five-eighths-inch to two-and-one-half-inch

Stab to base of front of neck, clearly post mortem.

Right eye — pulled out of socket, eyelids inverted, incision around inner aspect of eyelid

(not a wild hacking) muscles holding eye all disrupted, optical nerve to back of eye intact.

Not only did Chase use a knife to cut Evelyn Miroth's rectum, thrusting the blade back and forth while inside her (the sexual implication here being quite clear), but he sodomized her, as well. That which he found so difficult to achieve in life (having orgasms) with living women, he accomplished with the body of Evelyn Miroth. According to the report, the sperm found within her rectum was significant and could not have been from the night prior to her murder. When investigators interviewed her boyfriend, he said they never had anal intercourse, and that they did not have normal sex after the previous Monday evening.

At 11:05 a.m., Neone Grangaard sent her six-year-old

daughter, Tracy, over to the Miroth home to see what was keeping Jason. One can only imagine what she later thought, after discovering what was happening inside the home even as her child was pounding on the door, but as luck would have it, Richard Chase did not open it and invite her inside. After her daughter returned home, Ms. Grangaard made the following statement: "When Tracy came back, the station wagon was still there. And then, when I looked, it was still there, and then I got on the phone." No one answered Ms. Grangaard's call, and when she looked out her window immediately afterward, Meredith's car was gone. Chase, who had already robbed the deceased Daniel Meredith of his wallet and keys, would later explain he was interrupted by the child's arrival, and said, "somebody knocked at the door, so I took the baby and split."

Driving Meredith's car, witnesses said they saw the red station wagon driving through the neighborhood as Chase sought his escape. Understanding he was driving the stolen vehicle of a homicide victim, and that he needed to dump the car and return for his, he did so at the Sandpiper Apartments at 3535 Marconi Avenue. Prior to arriving at the Sandpiper Apartments, however, it nearly all came crashing down around him. Seventy-one-year-old Retta Scott had been shopping the morning of the murders, and only a few blocks away from Merrywood Drive. She would later tell investigators that by 9:30 a.m. she was at the Metropolitan Ski Shop at Marconi and Fair Oaks Boulevard. She then drove to Montgomery Ward, located in the Country Club

Center. She reported she drove on the north side of the parking lot (very close to where the lot dead-ends with Merrywood on the other side), headed to El Camino Avenue, "and drove west on El Camino Avenue, as she planned to go to a store on Del Paso Boulevard in north Sacramento." Richard Chase, carrying the partially mutilated body of twenty-two-month-old David Ferreira, was just now leaving the neighborhood streets behind him. "As she was driving west on El Camino," the report continued, "in the left lane, a Bright Red (capitalization theirs) station wagon pulled onto El Camino Avenue from Meadowbrook Way, directly in front of her vehicle, nearly colliding with her. She recalls being very angry and calling the driver of the vehicle a 'hoodlum' or something similar." Retta described the man as being "a WM (white male) twenty to forty years with long, scraggly hair." Once at the Sandpiper (and unlike the parking job he did with the Ranchero earlier that morning), Chase pulled perfectly into a proper space, and nothing seemed unusual as he exited the car. From this spot, Chase's apartment complex was about one hundred yards away. Prior to doing this, however, Chase most likely brought the body of the toddler to his apartment before walking back home. Being at home also meant he needed a ride back to the Country Club Center. Spotting the manager of the complex, he asked Don Tietjen if he had any work around the apartments he could do. When Tietjen said not at the moment, Chase bummed a cigarette from him and asked if he could give him a ride to "the Center." Tietjen again said no, explaining he didn't drive. Chase turned and walked away toward Watt avenue, where he headed south on foot to pick up the Ranchero. Tietjen later told investigators Chase looked perfectly normal.

Daniel Meredith's station wagon now abandoned at the Sandpiper Apartments

It must be remembered that while Richard Chase did bizarre things, and often looked mentally unbalanced due to his appearance, he was nevertheless aware he had committed murder and that it's against the mores of society to do such things, and he always attempted to conceal his actions to avoid arrest and prosecution. In this respect, Chase was killing and ordering his steps accordingly, so as to keep murdering for as long as he desired. To have remained so calm and collected while talking to Don Tietjen speaks of a cold-bloodedness that is both calculating and willful. In other words, Richard Chase was in complete control of his actions, regardless of the mental problems that were undeniably in his life.

Back at the Miroth residence, all was quiet and yet undiscovered, and Richard Chase was preoccupied with covering his tracks. Meanwhile, what must have been frustration quickly turned to apprehension for Neone Grangaard, as her calls went unanswered and there was no sign of anyone being at the Miroth home. Very concerned now, she and Tracy walked back over, and after ringing the doorbell, Grangaard said, she had her "daughter try the lock on the door, and it was locked." As Neone Grangaard stood there with her daughter, she peeked in the front window but didn't see anyone. She could tell the kitchen light was on, but no movement was seen wherever she looked, and no sounds were coming from the house. Mother and daughter then walked back home.

At 12:15, as the Grangaards were leaving, Neone Grangaard stopped to speak with neighbor Nancy Turner "about where Evelyn might be." Of course, Ms. Turner found it strange, so she decided to go over to the Miroth home with her son to see if she could learn anything. According to Grangaard, Nancy Turner "tried the front door, and then we went around to the back, and I stayed at the back door to keep the kids out, and her and her son entered ... she paused at the kitchen — in the kitchen to look into the bedroom in back, and she couldn't see anything in there. So, she proceeded through the kitchen and she went around the corner and she immediately turned and came back through the kitchen." Nancy Turner was not emotionally prepared to see the horror that greeted her as she entered the bedroom containing the mutilated body of Evelyn Miroth. Pushed into a mild state of shock, she told Grangaard, "It's Evelyn, and I think she's hurt, and there's blood all over." Turner also muttered the sheriff should be called. Ms. Grangaard was about to run over to her house for the number to the Sheriff's Department, but a Goodwill truck coming down the street saw there was some kind of trouble and stopped. When they were told what Nancy Turner had seen, they radioed the information to their dispatcher, who contacted the police.

Deputy Ivan Clark of the Sacramento County Sheriff's Department arrived at the Miroth residence at 12:43 p.m. and immediately spoke with Nancy Turner. Upon entering the home, Clark quickly found the bodies and then set out to secure the scene by keeping everyone out, while at the same time contacting dispatch for homicide detectives to begin heading for the scene. Although Deputy Clark was a "hardened" cop, those who saw him later spoke of how affected he was by the scene. Having worked the Wallin murder, as well, this was the second dose of horror he had to deal with this week. (Later, as Lieutenant Ray Biondi showed up with a host of investigators, he would allude to this in his remembrances, in that he noticed Deputy Clark's face "was an unusual pasty gray," before quickly adding that, "Whatever was inside had to be awful." It was at this time that Biondi also lamented the frustration felt by cops desperately trying to find killers who seem to be one step ahead of them: "We always knew where he *had* been, never where he was." When detectives Bill Roberts and Ken Baker showed up at the Merrywood investigation, as things began to unfold, they discovered some detective and patrol vehicles were blocking the street at the corner of Merrywood Drive and Highridge Drive, so they had to park about a block away. Roberts remembered it being foggy, and it was turning cold. When he saw Ivan Clark, he, too, could tell the veteran deputy was somewhat shaken by what he'd seen, adding "he was very ashen. ... " Roberts, who had graduated with Clark from the police academy, said, "He had the bad luck to get both the Wallin homicide and this one. He was a big guy, very solid, very intelligent.")

In any event, the first homicide investigator to respond to Ivan Clark's call for assistance was Detective Fred Homen, and soon, a flood of police and medical personnel was swarming over the Miroth residence, and methodically, they began their work. Detective Homen noted in his report that the Miroth phone "rang continuously" during this time. At some point during that terrible morning, Karen Ferreira received the call she never could have imagined. One investigator noted: "I advised Mrs. Ferreira that her sister-in-law was dead and that there were two other people, a male adult and an older child, who were also dead. She was advised that her child had not been found. At her request, I called her husband at work and requested that he respond to his sister's house, that there was a problem and he was needed. Mr. Ferreira stated that he would be here in ten minutes." The time now was 3:55 p.m. Shortly thereafter, Tony and Karen Ferreira, along with friends Phil and Lil Jarurn, arrived at 3207 Merrywood.

While the investigators wrestled with this latest scene of carnage, and the city of Sacramento was sent reeling for a second time in a week, Richard Chase returned home to indulge himself with the remains of the child. Long gone were the days of feasting on the blood and flesh of birds and dogs. Now, he was enjoying his own kind. The next morning, Chase would purchase and keep as a memento a copy of *The Sacramento Bee*, which described the Miroth/Meredith murders in great detail, with accompanying pictures of the victims.

Chapter Five

There's a Madman on the Loose

Richard Trenton Chase was getting away with murder. At least, in what may be accurately described as being, in the short-term. He has been described as crafty, calculating, cold-blooded, cruel, even diabolical, and all of these labels are true. But, he was also not very smart. He was smart enough to wear gloves as he entered homes for theft or murder, but rather dumb in that he was committing all his crimes within approximately a one-mile radius of his apartment. He was smart enough to park Mr. Meredith's car properly when he left it at the Sandpiper Apartments, but foolishly left the Ranchero parked oddly by the planter at Country Club Center, partially blocking a lane. It was pure luck he wasn't either ticketed or towed (in either case the police would have his name) while he was committing the slaughter less than two hundred feet away. Add to all of this his unquestioned mental illness (though legally sane, it must be remembered), and you have a recipe for disaster for Chase's career as a killer. This, of course, would give the police a slight edge when it came to apprehending him. But, the real question was how long would it take before he was caught and the murders would stop? As can be expected, the citizens of Sacramento, and especially those of east Sacramento, were shocked that something so heinous could be visited upon them. Many who owned guns kept them at the ready and purchased additional ammunition, and others, who didn't own any weapons at all, took the time to buy one. Fear was escalating in the community, and unless the person was apprehended, everyone expected the murdering to continue.

Thus far, the only thing the authorities knew for a certainty was that a twenty-something white male with long hair and looking rather scruffy was the person responsible for committing these murders, and that he no doubt lived very near to where the crimes were taking place. But, there were lots of young white males fitting that description in east Sacramento, and it would take the diligent leg work of all the detectives and patrol officers working overtime to catch this guy. It had been a terrible week, beginning with the Wallin killing, and now multiple homicides from what authorities correctly surmised was the same individual. No one would be getting much sleep, and everyone was hitting the streets in search of the leads they so desperately needed. It was classic police work, in that it required the same type of repetitive actions: canvassing neighborhoods, talking with everyone in the affected areas, and leaving no stone unturned. Amidst all of this organized but chaotic activity, they couldn't have known that things were about to go their way in little more than twenty-four hours.

While Merrywood Drive became a magnet for law enforcement, with police vehicles coming and going, and distraught neighbors watching from their driveways, Richard Chase went about his business of further mutilating the body of David Ferreira. In the privacy of his filthy apartment, he would cut off the head of the child and drink the blood, while eating portions of the body (brain matter). The apartment itself resembled a butcher's shop that was never cleaned, as there was blood everywhere. As such, it had been sometime since Chase had allowed anyone to come inside. Of course, he had no friends or usual visitors (and apparently his sister, Pam, was keeping her distance), so it was only his mom and dad who were forced to hand groceries and other items through a crack in the door. Later, those responsible for going over his place spoke of the stench of putrefaction, with practically no items or surfaces that were not stained by blood. When they looked in the refrigerator, Chase had pushed everything back on the top shelf to make room for a large item that police believe may have been the remains of the toddler. Because of a routine knock at the door by police as they were conducting a canvass of the area, Richard Chase decided to rid himself of the remains of David Ferreira. The dumping of the body, like the murders he'd committed, would be close to his apartment, and like the murders, he would not be caught in the act. His short reign of terror, however, was about to come to an abrupt end.

Within hours of the slaughter at the Miroth residence, the Sacramento County Sheriff's Department put out the following memo:

Operations Plan

East Area Saturation Patrol

Overview: Two recent homicides scenes, involving several victims, are believed to be connected, based on the suspect's method of operation. Both scenes are in relatively close geographical proximity and they occurred in the same general time frame. A patrol saturation effort will be implemented on 1-28-78.

Patrol Area: The area receiving saturation patrol is bounded by Auburn Boulevard and Edison Avenue on the north, Ethan Way on the west, the American River on the south, and Eastern Avenue and Estates Drive on the east. This area has been divided into fifteen sections, and each section will be patrolled by a one-officer unit. The attached map shows the boundaries of the patrol.

Time: The officer assigned to this saturation effort shall be in uniform for briefing at 0800 hours and within their assigned sector at approximately 0845 hours. They are to return to the office by approximately 0315 hours. This special patrol will be conducted until further notice.

Supervision: A patrol sergeant will be designated as the Field Supervisor of the saturation patrol. The sergeant will be responsible for assimilating current information which may be of assistance to the officers under his direction, for conducting briefing and for the regular distribution of rosters.

Aerial Detail: The aerial detail will provide coverage during the same hours being worked by radio units and will concentrate on the same patrol area.

Unit Designations: The radio units will be designated as Victor One through Victor Fifteen, which will coincide (with) their patrol sector assignments.

Background Information: The information available is currently as follows:

1-23-78 Monday 2630 Tioga Way, 187 of a WFA occurred generally between 1000 hours and 1300 hours. Victim shot with a .22-caliber automatic and mutilated with a knife.

A residence burglary also occurred on 1-23-78 at 2929 Burnece at approximately 1100 hours. A suspect description and composite is on the attached Crime Bulletin. The subject is wanted for questioning in the 187's.

1-27-78 Friday 3209 (sic) Merrywood, 187 of a WFA, WMA, a six-year-old child and possibly a two-year-old child occurred generally between 0900 hours and 1230 hours. The two-year-old is missing as of this date. Victims shot with a .22-caliber automatic and the female mutilated with a knife.

Mission: The mission of the units involved is to maintain a close patrol of the residential area of their sector. They are to make contact with and identify all subjects they observe, whenever this contact would appear reasonable to the particular officer. Since there is no description of the suspect, the officer involved should view this latitude widely. All individuals that cannot satisfy you regarding their reason for being in the area, or who are suspicious to you for any reason, should be F.I.'d. The sergeant assigned will have a camera available if a photo is necessary. Particular attention should be paid to walkers. The officers involved are requested to explain the reason for temporary detentions, at the appropriate time, in order to retain the confidence the legitimate citizens contacted. Officers should attempt to avoid involvement in incidents not related to the mission. Responding to burglaries in progress, suspicious subjects or vehicles, etc., are, of course, directly related to the mission.

The next morning, on the 28th, Chase's father called him from the Pantry Market, asking him if he needed anything. Richard said he didn't, and his father would later say he sounded normal. But Richard Chase was anything but normal, and soon the world would know the face and name of the most diabolical killer Sacramento had ever seen. And, the mammoth investigation that had seized the entire body of law enforcement was about to pay the ultimate of dividends.

What follows is the personal account of Detective Bill Roberts on the investigation and arrest of Richard Trenton Chase. Indeed, it would be three

Vampire

rookie detectives (Bill Roberts, Ken Baker, and Wayne Irey) who would play a pivotal role in the capture of the killer:

"The next day I was teamed up with Detective Carol Daly. She was an experienced detective and had worked child abuse, homicide, and other important cases. She was unalarming, soft-spoken, and very pretty, and it was easy for people to talk to her. We were assigned to start doing the background checks of our victims. What, if anything, did they have as a common denominator? We had checked several different angles. Were there school, church, shopping ties? Did they have any common friends? None of this was panning out. It seemed that victims from three different homicide scenes had no connection to each other. We got a radio call to 10-21 (phone) the command post. Detective Daly and I received information from Inspector Dave Goodman about a possible suspect named Richard T. Chase. He supposedly lived in the Marconi Avenue and Watt Avenue area. The inspector stated that a retired sergeant had his daughter phone in to report a strange meeting with someone at the Town and Country Shopping Center. Apparently, she recognized a disheveled, crazed man that was trying to talk to her as someone she went to high school with. She stated that a Richard Chase was the man, and she felt very uncomfortable around him at that time.

"I looked his name up in the phone book, and he had a listed address as 2934 Watt Avenue number 12. It was nearby, so Carol and I went to the location and made contact at Apartment number 12. The male

there wasn't Richard Chase and had no idea who he was. He had lived in this apartment for about three weeks. Carol and I went to the manager's apartment, only to find that no one was home. We couldn't get a forwarding address or further lead on Mr. Chase unless we would come back. I dropped Carol off at our command post, and I went downtown to start to compile more information on Richard Chase.

"I talked to Ray Biondi and told him I was going to do a workup on Richard T. Chase and that Detective Daly was dropped off at our area command post. I told him that the address checked negative for his living there, and it would need a re-contact with the apartment manager to see where Mr. Chase had moved. I went to our records section. It was a 'Sound Dex' records system. Everyone was placed on 6-inch-by-8-inch cards. Arrests, Reports, Contacts were all placed on these cards if it was a local county incident only. The city and state had different systems. When I first received Richard Trenton Chase's card, it showed marijuana arrests, and also an entry for a (5150 W&I) walk away from one of our local psychiatric hospitals. Of course, it gave his height and weight and other descriptors, but I was very interested in the fact that he also had two incidents involving .22-caliber pistols. I asked to have his folder pulled. It contained booking sheets, photos, and rap sheets. The first thing I did was look at the old booking photos. The very first one I picked up gave me a jolt. I couldn't believe that it resembled the sketch poster of what a witness described our suspect as looking like. I had a copy of the sketch in my folder and took it out.

It depicted a white male adult in his late twenties, early thirties with shoulder-length hair and clean shaved. The photo I was looking at of Chase during one of his bookings was that of a white male adult in his middle twenties, shoulder-length hair and a small mustache and goatee.

"I used a black marking pen to draw in a small mustache and goatee onto the sketch photo. It was close enough to make me excited. I even asked one of the ladies at the records counter what she thought of the comparison. Her first words were, 'Wow that looks really close.' I thought that this had to be the guy, but I calmed down long enough to do a further investigation. His folder contained a federal rap sheet that listed an arrest in Pyramid Lake, Nevada. I knew in my heart that Richard Trenton Chase was our man. A crazy, bizarre person, owns .22-caliber weapons, has been in psychiatric hospitals for violence, arrested covered in blood in the middle of the Nevada desert, identified by a witness as acting bizarre within a block of the Wallin homicide on the day of the homicide, and so similar to the sketch photo of our suspect. If my calculations were correct, he lived within a mile and a half of all of our crimes. This had to be him. One of the things I learned from other older cops is that coincidence is never coincidence when it comes to crimes. When things look like they fit together, they usually do. I did further workup on Chase. I ordered more current DMV photos from their law enforcement desk. I got several of all of the photos in his folder. I had copies made regarding any cases where arrests were made.

I made sure we had a current set of 'flats' of his fingerprints in our ID section. I ran a current DOJ rap sheet and also requested records to run a current federal rap sheet. Nowhere in our records section did it list parent's residence as being a current residence. We could only go on the DMV record that listed his most current address as 2934 Watt Avenue number 15.

"I kept thinking that can I really have the right guy? Some older detective should be getting this lead. I kept thinking, I know this is the guy, but at the same time I thought that maybe I'm just a little too new to be feeling this way. I went upstairs to the third floor and found Ray Biondi. I know I was very excited and was telling him that Chase was the guy. I spelled out all of what I had put together and where it came from. Ray was a calm person and said make him copies of all that stuff and put it in his basket. He said that the very person who had actually generated my lead on Chase was giving an in-person interview to Detective Irey. Biondi said we would wait to hear from Irey.

"In about thirty minutes, Detective Irey came into the homicide office and spoke to Biondi. I listened with hope that his interview would support my feeling that Chase was the guy. Irey then described that Nancy Holder encountered Richard Chase in the parking lot of the Pantry Market at the Town and Country Shopping Center. At first, she didn't recognize him, but she figured out that she knew him from high school days. She described him as disheveled, dried blood all over his shirt and orange ski parka. And,

a crazed, drugged look in his eyes. He tried to force himself into her car, but she locked the doors and drove off. She had seen him the same day as the Wallin homicide, whose residence was just over a fence separating the parking lot of Pantry Market from the home. She had brushed by death and didn't even know it. Her description of Chase was the same as Wallin neighbors gave to the strange prowler they had seen in the area the day Wallin was murdered.

"*Biondi was now a little more than interested. This was the best lead to date. He told us to make contact with Chase and see if he would come down to the office for a statement. I talked with Irey, and we agreed that we believed that we had identified the suspect. We asked Detective Ken Baker to come with us, since we felt that Chase was indeed the suspect everyone was looking for. He was sitting in a corner typing reports that he had gotten behind on. We all used typewriters and reports got behind when involved in something this massive. Baker objected to coming with us, and we both made some type of unkind remark that almost compelled him to come with us. Irey and I briefed Baker about why we wanted him to come with us. We all had belief in one another from being in patrol on the streets. We told him that Chase was unpredictable; we wanted enough backup if needed.*

"*I remember being excited on the way over to the apartment complex. We pulled into the back parking lot and parked in one of the overhead spaces. As we approached the apartments, one of us (I don't remember who) spotted the pickup truck that was just like the one listed as a possible suspect vehicle.*

It checked clear for any persons or any obvious signs of criminal activity. We left it there and went to the apartment manager's office. It was upstairs and in a row of apartments separate and next door to Chase's apartment. The female manager told us that Chase lived in apartment number 15 in the next row of apartments, downstairs and in the middle. Baker had stayed downstairs watching that apartment while Irey and I talked with the manager. She followed us downstairs and told us he was very strange and would not answer the door. She said that he would only talk to his mother through a crack in the door when she came to visit.

Baker positioned himself away from the door and to our right so he could observe the apartment window while Irey and I knocked on the front door. Nothing. We did it again a couple of more times, again with nothing. Baker said nothing was moving near the window. We didn't have our guns drawn but had our suit coats thrown back, and we at the ready. The manager, who was watching nearby, said, 'I told you he wouldn't answer.' She said that he must be home because his pickup truck was parked nearby. It was the same vehicle that we checked when we arrived earlier.

"*I went to the manager's apartment to use her phone. I had the most recent phone number of Chase, and I called it. After a couple of rings, someone picked up and said, 'Hello.' I asked if this was Richard, and he said, 'Yes.' I then made some small talk about how he had met me once before and told him my name 'Bill.' Without any more conversation, he hung up the phone.*

I told Irey, who went back to tell Baker, who continued to watch the apartment. I then called Lieutenant Biondi and told him what we had. I told him about the truck, the phone call, and what the manager said about him not opening the door. Biondi told me to stay put and he would send a marked unit and other detectives. I went downstairs and told Baker and Irey that the cavalry was on its way. The apartment to the right of Chase's was vacant. The windows were wide open, and there were no drapes covering the windows, and the lights were on. It had just been freshly painted that day. Baker got the passkey from the manager, and he let himself in and listened at a common wall. Irey and I were outside near Chase's front door and continued talking through the door. We continued to identify ourselves as deputies and the need to talk to him. Baker confirmed that he heard movement from inside Chase's apartment. Irey and I discussed exigent circumstances and if they existed due to the baby still being missing and not confirmed as a homicide victim. We chose to get further instructions from Lieutenant Biondi. We didn't want to screw this case up, but time was getting very precious if, in fact, the baby was still alive. We concocted a plan where we would very loudly tell Chase that we would be back as soon as we went and got a warrant, and then pretended to leave. Meanwhile, Baker was still inside the vacant apartment next door, and Irey walked with me to the end of the building, out of sight of Chase's apartment, and around the corner. Irey maintained vigil at one end and Baker at the other.

"Again, I went upstairs to the manager's apartment to phone Lieutenant Biondi and tell him what progress, or lack thereof, we had made. In those days, police communications was still in the dark ages. We didn't have portable radios, cell phones, text messaging, or anything called the Internet. Our cars had five channels for radio traffic: north of the river, south of the river, a records channel, a short-range car-to-car channel, and a data channel to dispatch patrol on calls. As I was on the phone with Biondi, the female manager SCREAMED, 'Your partners need help.' I raced down the stairs, taking them six or seven at a time, and made it around the corner with gun drawn, as I watched Irey pulling up a dirty, disheveled Richard Trenton Chase."

As Bill Roberts was talking on the phone, detectives Baker and Irey were waiting for Chase to make a move. Obviously believing the investigators had left, Chase stepped out of his apartment holding a "Mac Fries" box and would have headed towards the parking lot where his Ranchero was parked. However, he spotted Detective Irey, who had pressed himself up against an apartment about three doors up towards the parking lot, and for a second he appeared to be going back inside his place, but he then took off running down the narrow sidewalk attempting to reach Watt Avenue. Detective Baker later testified: "I jumped out of the doorway, ordered him to stop. I had my gun drawn. The subject turned, looked at me, and he was carrying a large cardboard box (this box contained bloody rags and papers, brain matter in an envelope, and David Ferreira's diaper pin). At that time, he threw the box at me. I had a flashlight in my hand. I was able to deflect the box, and as I deflected it downward, the subject charged me ... he tried to run over me, and I hit him. He flew in the air, and I came down on top of him." As Wayne Irey caught up with them, the two men were still struggling.

Irey, who'd already determined that if the baby was there he was going to kill him, found out the difference between someone like Richard Chase and the average person, including police officers. Describing what happened from the moment Chase decided to run, Irey said: "At the time, he's looking back over his shoulder as I'm chasing him. He gets down here to apartment 14 (next door), where Detective Baker was. ... Ken knocked him down, and then we jumped on him, wrestled around with him. ... his gun was in a holster underneath the jacket on his chest. I pulled my service revolver out and stuck it in his ear. I told him to quit fighting or I was going to blow his brains out ... well, he didn't quit fighting, and that's when I found out I'm not like him. Even though I believed it would have been a good shooting ... I couldn't kill him. Because the average person, cops included, are not like these people. He's a cold-blooded killer, and we aren't."

The box with its bloody contents, and the murder weapon Chase was carrying at the time of his arrest

As it turned out, a bullet in the ear wasn't necessary anyway, as Detective Baker pulled out his heavy, .45-caliber pistol and bashed Chase in the head. This action produced the necessary effect, and the killer was now in custody. One of the first things Chase said as they pulled him to his feet was, "Let me go, I've done nothing wrong." Another report has him saying: "I didn't do anything wrong. Who said I did anything wrong, did that lady hear me?" He also kept trying to get to his back pocket (at least three times), and the detectives soon discovered why: Chase was carrying in his hip pocket Daniel Meredith's wallet, containing his license, credit cards, and all of the other normal things people carry with them every day.

Although it was a vital piece of evidence, it was now just one of many, for within the "lair" Richard Chase called home, a ghastly scene awaited those officers about to enter. In just a few minutes, as Chase was being driven to the Sheriff's Department, he blurted out: "My apartment is a lot cleaner, isn't it? All I did in my apartment is kill a few dogs." Continuing now with the recollections of Bill Roberts:

"They had him cuffed behind his back, and Irey and Baker were both huffing and puffing, not from exhaustion, but from adrenalin. I asked if they were OK, and they said that they were. I saw this large cardboard box on the ground and looked into it. (There was a) bloody phone book, other rags and a plastic bucket. Chase had a large knot on his forehead, and I asked how he got that. Baker stated that he hit him with his .45 when Chase went for his gun. Baker then showed me the gun he had taken from Chase. Irey and I then walked Chase over to the end of the building where Irey had been hiding and began checking his clothing for any weapons or other evidence. Irey found property belonging to Mr. Meredith in Chase's back pocket. I was holding onto Chase while Irey had been doing the search. When he showed me Mr. Meredith's property and looked at me with a grin, I got this feeling like I had just hit a homerun in the bottom of the ninth. We got him!

"Baker was guarding the crime/arrest scene from apartment tenants, who had heard all the noise and possible scream from the manager. One of us told Baker about the property evidence we found on Chase. Baker had this big smile and acknowledged

the news with a head nod. Deputy Jim Kahlar drove his marked unit into the back of the apartment complex, and we put Chase in the backseat. Help was here, but we actually had the crazed serial killer in custody. Chase looked like he was on some downer drug, but he wasn't confused. He knew we were the cops, and he knew he had been caught. His manner was flat, no emotion, but his eyes were looking all over the place. What was he thinking of? I wondered if he saw Detective Carol Daly and I earlier in the day. It seemed in no time at all, the place was swarming with detectives and uniformed patrol officers. Lieutenant Biondi was there, and I remembered that I hadn't finished my phone call with him. I apologized, and he laughed and said it was OK since I got a little busy. Once the heavy-hitters started arriving and took over the scene, we just told Lieutenant Biondi what we did and how everything came into place. Detective Homen and Habacker and Sergeant Bevins were much more experienced detectives than we were.

"At the scene, everyone was extremely composed and all about business. All we would get was that occasional nod of the head from one of our fellow detectives or superiors. It felt good. The scene outside Chase's apartment was eerie. It was dark around us, but the light from the vacant apartment almost made it seem like daytime at the same time. I think we must have had our senses on high alert. I know it was cold that time of year, but I don't remember ever feeling that way. As we put Chase into the patrol car's rear seat, I remember seeing the manager. She

was talking to another detective, giving some kind of statement. I hoped that she was all right. She had just experienced the capture of a serial killer within feet of where she worked and lived."

As investigators entered the apartment of Richard Chase, the first thing they noticed was the smell of putrefaction, and blood was everywhere. In the bedroom was found a bloody plate on the bed, along with men's bloodstained clothing. Also found on the bed "were three brain particles." These, the report noted, were from the body of David Ferreira. A bloodstained hatchet was in the kitchen, and a bloody machete was found in a bedroom drawer. A large bloodstain was in the middle of the kitchen floor, and in the freezer they found a half-gallon container of animal meat consisting of "kidney, liver, or heart." Feces were found on the bedroom floor, and Chase had adorned the walls with pictures of human internal organs. "Reading material in the apartment included a book on totalitarianism, a book entitled 'Psychic People,' gun magazines, and psychology magazines. There were newspaper articles on violent deaths, and materials on Old West outlaws. Also, defendant's high school yearbooks." Inside the bathroom, blood was everywhere, too: "Entering the bathroom area, bloodstains were noted on the door leading to the bathroom, and the floor and walls. In the bathtub and tile around the bathtub, bloodstains were noted. Hair was seen in the bathtub and in the soap dish. In the medicine cabinet, a brown bag was observed. In opening the bag, hair was observed. Also in the cabinet was a plastic-type glass that had bloodstains inside. The Crest toothpaste containers had bloodstains on them."

"Lieutenant Biondi told me to get in the patrol car with Deputy Kahlar and take Chase downtown to headquarters and put him in one of the interview rooms. He and Detective Irey followed in Lieutenant Biondi's car. The trip downtown was uneventful, but what happened next still numbs me to this day. We got to 711 G Street and pulled up to the back door. There was no media, no patrol personnel or detectives. I took Chase out of the car and into the building. Lieutenant Biondi and Detective Irey joined me, and we took the elevator to the third floor. Our first floor was for patrol personnel and the public counter in the lobby. The second floor was for our communications and records personnel, and the fourth floor (we called it 'Mahogany Row') was for administration and executive personnel.

"I walked past the entrance to the detective division and down a hallway to the back of the division. The rear entrance was where we brought in people for questioning or arrest. We didn't parade them through the detective division, and besides the interview rooms were just inside the rear entrance. As I came around the corner and into the detective division with Chase being held by his arm and (the) cuffs, I couldn't believe my eyes. The entire division was standing there, on chairs, standing on desks, filling that entire division with people, an absolute flood of people, but completely quiet. No conversations, no noise of any kind, maybe a phone in the distance, but no one was speaking. Detective Irey and I put him

Vampire

into Interview Number 1 and locked the door. At that moment, I think I was in shock seeing all those guys and gals. It was a very proud moment for all of us. I remember Lieutenant Biondi making some sort of thank-you speech, and then we went into his office to find out what was next.

"Lieutenant Biondi told Irey and I that we would be the first to interview Chase, since we had made the arrest. Irey and I had made homicide arrests before as patrol deputies, but never did the interviews. We got all of our facts and times together and went in and talked to him. He wasn't cuffed any longer and sat there across from us with a deflated look. His body language was limp and laid back in the chair. I took several photos of him with our old Polaroid Land camera. We did that of almost all of our arrestees because we wanted colored, up-to-date photos for our mug books and 'punk' books. I took several extra because I knew that a few people would want one. These photos were instant, and we waited for them to develop, and put them on the back of blank cardboard created for listing the name and charges, etc. The old booking photos were in black and white, and you had to wait for the jail to complete one of their booking photo cycles before the large roll was sent out for processing. That was usually two days.

"Chase was different than any other suspect I had interviewed or interrogated. Usually, a suspect will display worry, defiance, hostility, or a certain (type) of smugness about them. Chase just sat there with a flat demeanor, acting like we were not even in the room. He had been in plenty of sessions with psychiatric

personnel and questioned by officers during prior arrests, so sitting in a room with someone questioning him was nothing new. Irey and I tried everything we knew to get him to open up. We did the overwhelming evidence talk, the 'we know you did it, but why' speech, and the good cop-bad cop, where I yelled at him and Irey spoke to him as a friend. He did talk to us, but it was only to answer what questions he wanted to answer. Many questions just simply drew a stare and silence. We sat there not saying a thing, hoping that it would make him uncomfortable and he would speak to break the silence. Nothing! We were probably more uncomfortable than he was. We asked Lieutenant Biondi to send in the experienced homicide interviewers because we didn't think we were doing a good enough job. He assured us that we did just fine but did send in another team of investigators. Eventually, they, too, never received any useful information or admission from Chase.

"We spent the rest of the evening doing our typed reports. At the end of the night at about midnight, we went to a place called Zelda's for a nightcap and slice of pizza. It was a cop hangout close to the headquarters. I remember that we had just sat down and were waiting for a few more guys to join us when the phone call came in. The EAR had just struck, this time twin sisters were the victims. That was it, no drink, and no pizza, just a late response to another EAR crime scene.

"Later in our careers, we joked about being 'Once Famous Detectives.' It didn't matter what you had done the day before, it was always what you were

doing today that mattered to your victims and your contemporaries."

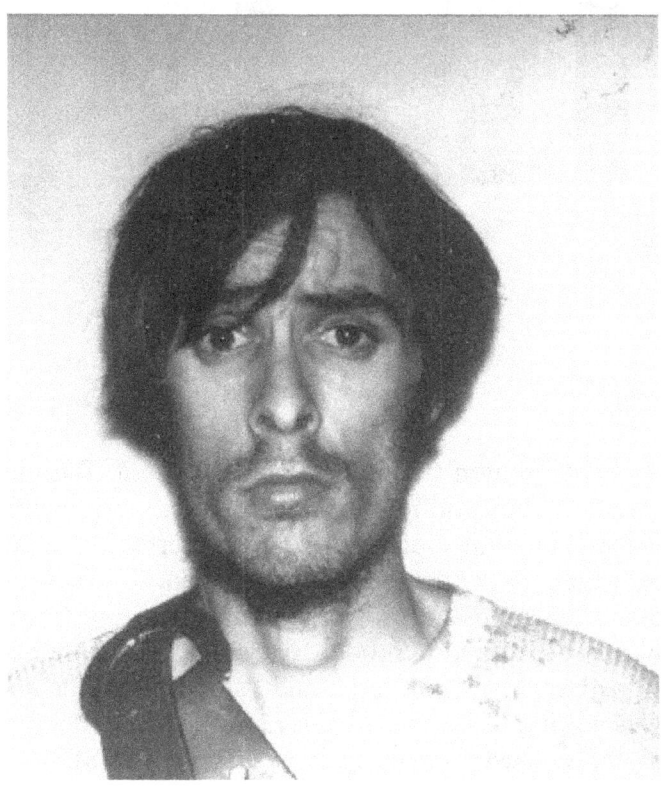

Chase mug shot

Chase and his new orange jacket

Richard Trenton Chase had been captured. Without question, they had in their midst the one responsible for a brief, but diabolical reign of terror the likes of which Sacramento had never seen. There were many questions needing to be answered, but Chase was not in a talking mood. By 7:14 p.m., Chase had signed a waiver stating he understood his rights and was willing to speak with the investigators. That first night, at least four detectives (in two shifts) spent several hours grilling the killer, but Chase was not about to incriminate himself in the Miroth, Wallin, or Griffin homicides; and of course, he denied having anything to do with the missing baby, David Ferreira. He would admit to the killing of dogs, but nothing more. The evidence against Chase was overwhelming (the .22 Luger pistol, for example, was quickly matched to all six murders), but no matter how long the detectives pressed him in these initial interviews, he would not admit to killing humans.

The holster Chase wanted to keep wearing during his interrogation

The oddities of Richard Chase, however, came quickly to the surface. One such oddity was when a detective decided to have Chase remove the now-empty shoulder holster he was still wearing. Upon hearing this, Chase "manifested great anxiety, (saying) it makes me feel better, it makes me feel comfortable ... can't I just hang onto it?" During the sessions with detectives Daly and Bevins, Chase, they said, was "very composed," and when they pressed him about the murders and specifically about the location of David Ferreira, he continued to deny involvement. But when they presented him with evidence that linked him to the crimes (and Chase knew the evidence connected him), he said he was "being framed" by the Italians. When asked whether he had been eating the flesh of his victims and drinking their blood, Chase said, "You're crazy ... I haven't ... I'm not mixed up in anything like that." When they asked if he thought it was wrong to eat people, Chase responded, "the Nazis ate a lot." Not only was Chase denying his involvement in the murders, but he offered what he thought were reasonable denials: "My parents didn't bring me up that way. I wouldn't do anything like that ... (you have) the wrong guy ... it wasn't me ... no shit ... I didn't do it." In an apparent switch from just denying the crimes, Chase began to speculate who might be responsible by saying he saw "a blond guy (who) had on an orange coat ... walking ... towards Country Club Center." Chase also mentioned, "Somebody's been coming in and out of my apartment."

Chase's first night in jail was an eye-opener as to

what the authorities would have to do just to keep him alive while in their care. Sitting in the Sacramento County Jail (a jail housing up to six hundred inmates), Richard Chase was a bizarre oddity. The prisoners on the floor, fully aware of their new guest, urinated in cups and passed them down to those housed in the cells next to Chase, and these emissaries did their best to hurl the contents on him. Some said feces were tossed in his cell, too. These same prisoners were very vocal in their promises to the jailors that if they would just turn Chase over to them, he'd be killed. Some of these hardened individuals spoke of not being able to sleep because of what Richard Chase had done. Very shortly, Chase was moved to a single cell on "3 south."

On Sunday morning, doctors True and Whipple interviewed their subject for two to three hours. Although tense and hesitant, Chase did tell them some things about his childhood, high school experiences with girls, and his involvement with "track and cross country." They noted, however, that he was "vague about having a psychiatric history." At one point, Doctor True asked him what was on his mind. Chase said "normal things," and when pressed about what was "on the screen of his mind," he said, "an exploding 747 jetliner." Chase also spoke of seeing lights in the sky "that might be UFO's, maybe from Mars." Chase rambled on about being Jewish (untrue), about how a gang of Italians had beaten him up, and other strange things.

Although Chase didn't worry any longer about his mother or another family member poisoning him, there were times that Chase's eating habits were erratic in jail, and he believed someone was trying to poison him. Chase, being represented by Farris Salamy (his public defender), instructed his investigator to have the food Chase gave him tested; this was done at the Sacramento County District Attorney's Crime Lab, and the results, when returned, were negative. An interesting aside, Farris Salamy told the author that Chase's demeanor rarely changed throughout the time he worked with him; that is, he was often withdrawn and uncommunicative. However, if there was a situation requiring him to be examined by a regular doctor, he would jump at the chance, such was his desire to find a "cure" for those things he perceived were ailing him. With all the evidence against Richard Chase, Salamy knew the battle to defend his client would be uphill all the way. The State of California vs. Richard Chase would prove to be one of the more momentous cases the state had ever tried, and for Farris Salamy, the most bizarre. Chase's only chance of escaping the death penalty would be found in a verdict of not guilty by reason of insanity. The prosecution, led by Ronald W. Tochterman and Deputy Al Locher, would do everything within its power to prove Chase was, in fact, sane when he committed these murders. No matter what the public believed constituted "crazy," there is a difference between a person being mentally disturbed and legally insane. And, it would be in this, the arena of his mental capacity at the time of the murders, that would decide whether Richard Chase would live or be put to death for his crimes.

Chapter Six

For All the World to See

Soon after the capture of Richard Chase, when the background of this strange individual started to emerge, it wasn't long before the labels "Dracula" and "vampire" were tossed about by the public when referring to him. Of course, he picked up the name Dracula while in Beverly Manor for his habit of biting the heads off of birds "and eating them raw." In light of the diabolical nature of the crimes, there was little else to call him. The January 31, 1978, edition of *The Sacramento Union* ran the following headline on page one, section one:

They called him 'the vampire'

Arthur Davis, identified as "supervising licensed vocational nurse" in the article, felt Chase was a real danger and believed he needed to be at a "stricter state institution, (adding) Chase was there from about August to December of 1976. He was released before I left in December and I — and others on the staff — were angry at the administration because we believed he was dangerous." Davis readily admitted Chase was referred to as "the vampire" by staff, such was his reputation. In fact, Chase's penchant for birds would continue while in jail. According to one report, Chase was in the chow line when one of the workers joked about food: "I bet this is a little different than what you usually eat," to which Chase replied, "Do we have any birds?" Richard Chase, the orderly said, was not joking.

While Chase languished in jail, often pulling the covers up over his head as guards passed his cell, the law enforcement community was using bloodhounds in the hunt for twenty-two-month-old David Ferreira, in what turned out to be a fruitless search for his body. Regrettably, the dog teams would come to within several hundred feet of where Chase had placed the remains, but that discovery was almost two months away. In the meantime, Chase would be charged with five counts of murder (with a sixth an obvious foregone conclusion once the baby was found), and the court-appointed doctors would be peering into the dark places of Richard Chase.

Vampire

The "Mac Fries" box containing the body of the child

On March 24, 1978, the body of David Ferreira was discovered. A janitor at the Arcade Wesleyan Church at 3532 Whitney Avenue (Whitney and Watt intersect) found a McDonald's "Mac Fries" box behind a gate that is normally locked. This is an area where the L-shaped church building T-bones against another building, and this space is church property. When the janitor saw the box and smelled the putrefaction, he knew something was dead inside. The partially mummified remains of David Ferreira had, at last, been found, and soon this crime scene would be swarming with investigators, evidence teams, and even the television news crews who were salivating to get a look at the macabre discovery. At one point, Lieutenant Biondi, believing he had the press corralled so they could conduct their work without prying eyes (and television cameras), discovered a camera crew setting up their equipment on the rooftop of the adjacent building so they could film the activities of those who were carefully reclaiming the remains of the toddler. This was cured when the homicide commander ordered his team to drape a sheet over top the area, thereby denying them the shot they so desperately wanted. That they (the media) wanted to intrude at such a moment, even before the parents, Tony and Karen Ferreira, had been informed, must have been galling indeed.

The autopsy of the child would accurately define for authorities what were the injuries to the boy, and they are as follows:

GSW (gunshot wound) to right side of head, passing through brain, exiting left side of head.

Several stab and incised wounds to the rear of the skull, knocking holes in the rear of the skull, the largest two-and-one-half-inches long.

Cutting from the scrotum through the rectal area, up to the sacrum (basically, cutting through the entire cleft of the buttocks).

Gaping wound to the chest and abdomen, ribs three through ten being broken.

Decapitation, cutting through the second cervical vertebrae.

During the autopsy, as they removed the child from the box, they found a set of keys. These keys, to no one's surprise, belonged to the deceased Daniel Meredith and fit his fire-engine-red station wagon.

The discovery of the body of their child was a crushing blow to Tony and Karen Ferreira. As with all families of the missing, there is always the chance, however remote, that their loved one will return someday, and death takes this away from them. When this occurs, there is very little one can say to comfort them.

In May of 1978, Chase had already been examined by four doctors, and all four declared him competent to stand trial. Chase, who had written a rambling statement as to why he pled not guilty by reason of "temporary" insanity, said, "Now that I have pled not guilty by reason of temporary insanity, I demand transportation to Vacaville Medical facility on the orders of Mr. Salami (sic) and my father, who are hiring a pulmonary embolus specialist to conduct pulmonary angiograms and file them as documentary evidence," according to *The Sacramento Bee*, May 23, 1978. In June, two psychiatrists were appointed by the court to evaluate Richard Chase as to his sanity. These sessions would not be beneficial to the defense, for while they clearly showed mental impairment, imbalance, and even illness, it did not show Chase to be unaware of his actions while committing murder. Their description of Chase would, in fact, differ from all earlier diagnoses declaring him to be schizophrenic (one would say he was, but still was responsible for his actions, the other rejected that diagnosis entirely), and this, too, would be welcome news for the prosecution. What follows are excerpts of these evaluations, beginning with Doctor Theodore M. Odland:

"In the sexual area, his sex education was a course in psychology at American River College. He began masturbation in the seventh or eighth grade and doesn't like it because it can cause sickness and weakness; he has abstained for the past several months, as he feels it may be contributing to his present weakness ... He has had limited heterosexual experience with intercourse and oral sex; he doesn't much care for it, as 'it's not worth it, I guess.'" Chase also discussed his problems maintaining an erection, and he denied ever having sex with animals or participating in homosexual activity. When it came time to discuss the murders, the early interviews were filled with statements from Chase that he couldn't remember the murders. And then, he began to open up a little: "After repeated requests to return to the offenses, he said, 'they were just ... it could have been someone else ... I don't remember who they were ... because I was sick, poisoned by iodine or mercury, I can't stand it, I can't get away from it.' ... He then rambled on some more, saying the offenses occurred over a 'couple of weeks' period' and that 'knives and guns were used.' He then said, 'I don't really remember anything about it. I was trying to get free of Poison Place and go live with my grandmother's relatives. The car had broken down, and I had no money, so I walked in someone's house and killed them.'" Chase also admitted killing a cat he once had as a pet. He happened to see a story on television about a cat receiving medical care he believed exceeded his own. Angered, he got up, grabbed the cat and went outside and killed it. He then drank some of its blood.

Of course, the cat was but the first of the animal killings. "He rambled on about putting a cup by the bullet holes in the animals to catch the blood," the report continued. "He saw on television and read in a book that poisons will clot the blood and make it disappear. Regarding the blood drinking not helping, he said, 'I couldn't cope with the world anymore because every time I tried to get up and act like a human being, I couldn't because of the weakness. I went on welfare and got in Beverly Manor. So, now I've got a trial pending, I guess." Concerning mental illness, Chase said: "Mental disease makes me get dizzy and lose my sense of reality over some kind ... it puts me to sleep, kind of." Chase then admitted "he was mentally ill when he killed the people, and when asked specifically about carrying the baby's body, he said 'some kind of blackout, I guess.'" When asked how he felt about killing the people, he said, "It was not fair to kill those people. I could have tried medical places out of town, but I went to a lot of places and couldn't find any help."

Doctor Odland, believing Chase was in fact schizophrenic but responsible for his actions, sums up his professional opinion of the killer with the following words — words that would do nothing but bolster the case for the prosecution:

"He was oriented in all three spheres and showed no gross memory loss, except for the killings, and my opinion is that this does not represent organic brain damage. His affect was flat and his associations were frequently loose. His affect was at times inappropriate to the thought content ... He described a vast persecutory delusionary system, which is organized and of long duration and involves systematic poisoning of him. He has many somatic delusions, including 'my heart stopped beating, I do not have a heart, my pulmonary artery has been stolen, my blood is not circulating, and poisoning is causing my stomach to grow backward' ... My opinion is that Richard was seeking relief from intolerable distress associated with his belief that he was being poisoned to death, and that his belief was due to a severe chronic mental disorder. He believed that drinking blood was a possible solution to save him from certain death. He understood that he was killing people and that it was wrong to kill people."

Doctor Alfred P. French, who conducted five interviews with Chase between June 16 and July 20, 1978, would be just as damning in his evaluation of the killer as was the report of Doctor Odland:

"Your Honor,

"Pursuant to your appointment of June 13, 1978, I interviewed Mr. Chase at the Sacramento County

Jail on June 16, June 20, June 26, July 6, and July 20, 1978. These interviews varied in length from thirty minutes (one interview) to one hour and fifteen minutes (one interview). The other three interviews were approximately forty-five minutes in length.

"QUESTION ADDRESSED AND OPINION: Was Richard Chase sane at the time of the commission of the offense for which he is charged?

"Mr. Chase has not discussed with me the events in question. While I have repeatedly asked him about the events in question on different occasions, he has repeatedly stated that he does not remember about them, although he stated in one case that 'I didn't kill anybody — just a few people.' My opinion is, therefore, based on indirect evidence, which I will present in detail below.

"On the basis of my five interviews and a careful review of the extensive written records and tape-recorded conversations, it is my opinion that the information available to me permits only one conclusion: Mr. Chase was sane at the time of the offenses, that he was capable of knowing and understanding the nature and quality of his acts, and that he was capable of knowing and understanding that his acts were wrong.

"BASIS FOR THE OPINION: The major bases for my opinion are as follows:

"(1) Absence of any evidence whatsoever, in my interviews, that this man is a schizophrenic;

"(2) A statement by Mr. Chase that he did, in fact, kill some people;

"(3) A distinct change in Mr. Chase's manner as we approached discussion of the sensitive areas. At this point, he consistently became cautious, withdrawn, evasive, and he refused to discuss matters;

"(4) Clear evidence that Mr. Chase has a well-developed sense of right and wrong with respect with how he, himself, should be treated (specifically, he has a clear sense that he should have an angiogram, that he should be moved to a hospital, that he should have been given blood or blood products, that his car should be cared for, etc.);

"(5) Clear evidence that Mr. Chase performed murders precisely because he was aware of the nature and quality of his acts, i.e. that destruction of these lives would make it possible for him to obtain blood and, apparently, other sources of gratification. To take the other side of the question, I find no evidence in the records or in my own interviews that Mr. Chase has been, at any time, incapable of knowing or understanding the nature and quality of his acts or incapable of knowing or understanding that his acts were wrong."

It was exactly what the prosecution expected and wanted from the psychiatric evaluations, and the case against Richard Chase solidified and was now moving in the state's direction. It didn't matter if Chase was mentally disturbed (who could deny this?), but understanding what his actions meant, and his desire to keep his actions a secret, did not speak of legal insanity, and this gave Farris Salamy an even greater mountain to climb. Saving his client's life would now be far more difficult.

Doctor French had other findings, as well: "As to abnormal behaviors while being interviewed, Chase had none." It was also noted that his manner of speech "is slow and cautious, with a soft voice." Chase's intellectual functioning was deemed normal, as he "expressed himself in sentences of normal length and complexity with no apparent difficulty, and I had no impression that this man is mentally retarded." His mental judgment was not impaired either, as Doctor French noted: "A number of hypothetical problem situations were presented. Mr. Chase responded to these hypothetical problems in what I considered to be a normal manner, demonstrating a variety of problem-solving maneuvers."

Concerning Richard Chase's need for blood, Doctor French had this to say: "Mr. Chase discussed his concern about his health and his attempt to repair his body through the ingestion of blood. This he attempted to do by ingesting the blood of rabbits and dogs. However, he did not obtain the desired results of improved health and attributed this failure to diseased animals. With respect to the entire matter, Mr. Chase, at one point, commented that it was 'a mistake' in that he should have simply gone directly to a blood bank."

Reversing the earlier diagnosis of schizophrenia, saying his findings demonstrated that Chase did not meet the criteria of such a diagnosis as outlined by the American Psychiatric Association's Diagnostic and Statistical Manual, the doctor wrote: "In my opinion, the cardinal finding of schizophrenia, namely the involuntary and uncontrollable disruption of the normal flow of thought process, is nowhere evident in this case. Furthermore, Mr. Chase repeatedly (said) to me, and to one other interviewer (conversation with ADA), specifically denied psychotic symptomatology. In my opinion, two diagnoses are merited: 297.9, other paranoid state, and 301.7, antisocial personality. For completeness, 307.3, adjustment reaction to adult life, is currently appropriate as Mr. Chase confronts a difficult situation. However, I will not discuss 307.3 further."

He sums up his evaluation by stating: "Of particular importance in this case is the evidence that Mr. Chase is in conflict with society, grossly selfish and callous, and apparently unable to feel guilt. Furthermore, he clearly tends to blame others and does his best to offer plausible rationalizations for his behavior. In my opinion, the behaviors in question resulted from the simultaneous presence of a delusional system and gross callous selfishness. Somatic delusions in themselves are by no means uncommon. Antisocial personality pattern is quite common. In this case, we are dealing with simultaneous presence of both conditions."

Buried within one of the many Q & A sessions Chase had was the acknowledgement of the real reason he took the body of David Ferreira: "'Cause I ... needed something to eat."

Farris Salamy, understanding it would be next to impossible for Richard Chase to obtain a fair trial in Sacramento, petitioned the court for a change of venue. This was both reasonable to the defense and unavoidable to the prosecution. Venue change was granted, and the trial was moved over one hundred miles south to Santa Clara County. Of course, the good people of Santa Clara had also heard of the deeds of Richard Trenton Chase, and while they didn't experience the fear of his brief reign of terror, it made jury selection interesting, to say the least.

On January 2, 1979, Richard Chase went on trial for the murders he'd committed, and Chief Assistant District Attorney Ronald Tochterman, with a singular determination, had but one true goal: to prove Chase was legally sane at the time of the killings. Tochterman, a brilliant prosecutor, had been living with the case for over a year now, and his preparation to try it left no stone unturned. He knew Chase was sane when he killed, and he was going to convince a jury of it, as well. According to his deputy district attorney, Al Locher, "Ron only knew one way to play the game: full press. There was no hiding the ball. He believed in just overwhelming the opposition, (Biondi and Hecox, *Dracula Killer*)."

Farris Salamy understood that if he could just get a verdict of not guilty by reason of insanity, he would have done an excellent job for his client. It was an uphill battle, and after the evaluations by doctors Odland and French, considered now to be next to impossible. And, if this could not be achieved, then he would press for a verdict of guilty of murder in the second degree, which would at least save Chase from the death house. But Ronald Tochterman was not about to see such a miscarriage of justice happen. The trial, itself, would present a sea of evidence pointing to Richard Chase, and it welcomed the testimony of many people, including the living victims of his rampage, like Carol Griffin, David Wallin, Nancy Holden (who saw Chase very close to the time Teresa Wallin was murdered), and others, oddly drawn together because of the slaughtering of their loved ones by the hands of Richard Chase.

In what may have been a surprise to some, Chase took the stand and admitted to murdering people and drinking their blood. He seemed to remember more about the murder of Teresa Wallin, but said he didn't remember much from the Miroth/Meredith killings. He also talked about his own problems, but none of this mattered to those who heard him, and none of this had anything to do with the direction the trial was going. On May 8, 1979, the jury, having found Chase to be sane at the times of the crimes, took less than five hours to decide his fate. When the jury was returned and the verdict read, Richard Chase was convicted of six counts of murder in the first degree. Ronald Tochterman, who had reminded the jury that "these murders were not ordinary or common; they betrayed a depravity that is so great that the level of reprehensibility manifested is difficult to imagine — almost beyond human conception or imagination," must have been exceedingly pleased.

Farris Salamy could not have been all that surprised. Still, there was hope, he reasoned, that perhaps at the sentencing hearing, the judge might give his client life in prison. But when the matter was taken up in court a week later, the sentence was death. Although Chase took the stand once again and begged for mercy, stating, "I beg for another chance to survive in the hope to make compensation for the families," adding, "I was a good person, although weak in heart and mind," this did not produce the mercy he was looking for. Farris Salamy, a good man and as diligent in his preparation for the trial as Ronald Tochterman, could not save Richard Chase from the sentence almost everyone believed he deserved.

There were other victims, as well: The family of Richard Chase was devastated by the verdict, the murders he'd committed, and the utter destruction of his life. Speaking to a reporter from *The Sacramento Bee*, Chase's father, while weeping openly, said: "Society will kill my son. I think I've known that from the start. And, maybe it's right, I don't know. There isn't a day goes by that I don't think about those people he killed ... I've cried a lot over the past year. I don't know whether it's been more for those people than for Rick."

Kevin Sullivan

Epilogue

Richard Chase was sent to San Quentin Penitentiary to await his end in the gas chamber. Of course, he was in California, a state where the condemned may die of old age before the poisoned pellets drop, so it was anyone's guess as to when that would occur. Isolated on Death Row, in cell 2 N, Richard Chase was as strange here as he was anywhere. As strange as Chase was, however, he had a plan, although we cannot determine exactly what his true intentions were in carrying out that plan. What is known is that at some point in the early morning hours of December 26, 1980, Chase swallowed a number of pills he'd been secretly stashing away instead of taking them as they were dispensed to him. Doing this, I was informed, was referred to as "cheeking" your meds. The guard who looked in on him around 8:00 a.m. said nothing appeared unusual, as Chase was lying on his bunk. But, when he checked again at 11:05 a.m., Chase was lying on his stomach, his legs were hanging off the bed, his face was buried into the mattress, and he appeared to not be breathing.

At that time, Officer Graham pulled Chase outside of

his cell and quickly determined he was dead. Chase was wearing blue jeans, a pull-over sweater, and tennis shoes. Leaving him lying on his left side on the concrete floor, the officer stopped any activity around the body and waited for others to arrive. The autopsy confirmed Chase had killed himself by an overdose of Sinequan, a thrice-daily prescribed medicine for depression. His death came three days short of the third anniversary of the murder of Ambrose Griffin. And while his death certificate states "suicide," some believe that Richard Chase was merely trying to cure himself once and for all of the ills he believed were plaguing him. The only thing that was certain was that the man dubbed "the Vampire of Sacramento" was now dead.

Acknowledgements

While almost everything contained within the covers of this book came from the official record, there were numerous people involved in helping me along the way as the process unfolded. The creation of a book does not happen without this help, and in this spirit, I would like to thank the following persons: Retired Detective William Roberts, one of the three arresting officers who brought Richard Chase's brief reign of terror to an end and brought relief to their jittery fellow Sacramentans. From the moment Bill answered my e-mail, he was on board with the project and ready to help in any way possible. That help came first in a file of the case he mailed to me containing photographs, newspaper articles, and other useful information I was grateful to receive. And then, during my visit to Sacramento, Bill was very gracious to drive me around the area where Chase committed his crimes, while explaining what it was like during that time. Without question, Bill's help was beneficial beyond words.

I would also like to thank Albert Locher and his staff at the office of the Sacramento County District

Attorney, for allowing my wife and me to occupy a spare office for the better part of a day while I waded through fourteen file boxes related to the case. Not only this, but each time I've contacted him with questions, or when I needed additional clarification and guidance through the labyrinth of facts contained in the official record, he was always quick to respond, and his answers were always helpful.

I would also like to thank: Frank Davidson, CSI officer with the Sacramento County Sheriff's Department, who worked the Teresa Wallin and Miroth murders; Retired Detective Ken Baker, also an arresting officer of Richard Chase, for his input into those days; Leonard Frizzi, former teacher at Mira Loma High School, who knew Richard Chase and had him as a student for one day, before Richard dropped his class; Deputy Jason Ramos, Sheriff's Spokesman for the Sacramento County Sheriff's Department; Michael Gillman of the Sacramento Public Library; Farris N. Salamy, attorney for Richard Chase; and others who remain nameless, but nevertheless aided me in my search for information.

And of course, I want to thank my wife, Linda, who has always been an integral part of my work. Not only does she accompany me on every research trip (once I have it in my head that a particular book must be written!), but she's always there to listen to my ideas and give me the appropriate advice, which helps keep me on track. As always, I'm eternally grateful for all that you do!

About The Author

A writer of history and true crime, Kevin M. Sullivan is the author of nine books, a former investigative journalist for both print and online media, and is a recognized authority on serial sex killer, Ted Bundy. Indeed, his "break out" book, *The Bundy Murders: A Comprehensive History*, published by McFarland in 2009, was the catalyst that brought him much attention in the true crime world, leading to numerous radio programs and contacts from documentarians both here in the United States and the United Kingdom. Portions of this work also appear in the college textbook, Abnormal Psychology: Clinical Perspectives on Psychological Disorders, published by McGraw-Hill in November 2012.

Kevin Sullivan

Thank you for reading *Vampire*. Word-of-mouth is crucial to the success of any author. If you enjoyed *Vampire* then I'd appreciate it if you provided an honest review at http://wildbluepress.com/VampireReviews.

You can sign up for advance notice of new releases at: http://wildbluepress.com/AdvanceNotice

Thank you for your interest in my books,

Kevin Sullivan

Kevin Sullivan

Other WildBlue Press Books
By Kevin Sullivan

KENTUCKY BLOODBATH: *Ten Bizarre Tales of Murder From the Bluegrass State*
http://wbp.bz/kb

THE TRAIL OF TED BUNDY:
Digging Up The Untold Stories
http://wbp.bz/trailbundy

THE BUNDY SECRETS: *Hidden Files On America's Worst Serial Killer*
http://wbp.bz/bundysecrets

See even more at:
http://wbp.bz/tc

More True Crime You'll Love From WildBlue Press

BOGEYMAN: He Was Every Parent's Nightmare by Steve Jackson
"A master class in true crime reporting. He writes with both muscle and heart." (Gregg Olsen, New York Time bestselling author). A national true crime bestseller about the efforts of tenacious Texas lawmen to solve the cold case murders of three little girls and hold their killer accountable for his horrific crimes by New York Times bestselling author Steve Jackson. *"Absorbing and haunting!"* (Ron Franscell, national bestselling author and journalist)

wbp.bz/bogeyman

REPEAT OFFENDER by Bradley Nickell
"Best True Crime Book of 2015" (Suspense Magazine) A "Sin City" cop recounts his efforts to catch one of the most prolific criminals to ever walk the neon-lit streets of Las Vegas. *"If you like mayhem, madness, and suspense, Repeat Offender is the book to read."* (Aphrodite Jones, New York Times bestselling author)

wbp.bz/ro

DADDY'S LITTLE SECRET by Denise Wallace
"An engrossing true story." (John Ferak, bestselling author of Failure Of Justice, Body Of Proof, and Dixie's Last Stand) Daddy's Little Secret is the poignant true crime story about a daughter who, upon her father's murder, learns of his secret double-life. She had looked the other way about other hidden facets of his life - deadly secrets that could help his killer escape the death penalty, should she come forward.

wbp.bz/dls

BODY OF PROOF by John Ferak
"A superbly crafted tale of murder and mystery." – (Jim Hollock, author of award-winning BORN TO LOSE) When Jessica O'Grady, a tall, starry-eyed Omaha co-ed, disappeared in May 2006, leaving behind only a blood-stained mattress, her "Mr. Right," Christopher Edwards, became the suspect. Forensic evidence gathered by CSI stalwart Dave Kofoed, a man driven to solve high-profile murders, was used to convict Edwards. But was the evidence tainted? A true crime thriller written by bestselling author and award-winning journalist John Ferak.

wbp.bz/bop

www.ingramcontent.com/pod-product-compliance
Lightning Source LLC
Chambersburg PA
CBHW071716020426
42333CB00017B/2288